SENSATIONAL SCRAPBOOK LAYOUTS & MORE™

EDITED BY TANYA FOX

HOUSE of
WHITE
BIRCHES

PUBLISHERS
SINCE 1947

D1377921

Sensational Scrapbook Layouts & More™

Copyright © 2007 DRG, 306 East Parr Road, Berne, IN 46711.
All rights reserved. This publication may not be reproduced in
part or in whole without written permission from the publisher.

EDITOR	Tanya Fox
ART DIRECTOR	Brad Snow
PUBLISHING SERVICES DIRECTOR	Brenda Gallmeyer
ASSOCIATE EDITOR	Sue Reeves
ASSISTANT ART DIRECTOR	Nick Pierce
COPY SUPERVISOR	Michelle Beck
COPY EDITORS	Kim English, Mary O'Donnell
TECHNICAL EDITOR	Läna Shurb
PHOTOGRAPHY SUPERVISOR	Tammy Christian
PHOTOGRAPHY	Don Clark, Matthew Owen, Jackie Schaffel
PHOTOGRAPHY STYLISTS	Tammy Nussbaum, Tammy Smith
GRAPHIC ARTS SUPERVISOR	Ronda Bechinski
GRAPHIC ARTIST	Erin Augsburger, Pam Gregory
PRODUCTION ASSISTANTS	Marj Morgan
TECHNICAL ARTISTS	Marla Freeman
PUBLISHING DIRECTOR	David J. McKee
BOOK MARKETING DIRECTOR	Dwight Seward

Printed in China
First Printing: 2007
Library of Congress Control Number: 2006926953
Hard Cover ISBN: 978-1-59217-146-0
Soft Cover ISBN: 978-1-59217-147-7

1 2 3 4 5 6 7 8 9

Every effort has been made to ensure the accuracy and completeness of the instructions in this book. However, we cannot be responsible for human error or for the results when using materials other than those specified in the instructions, or for variations in individual work.

WELCOME

My love of scrapbooking began years ago when I was expecting my oldest daughter. Creating beautiful layouts to capture all those wonderful "firsts" in her life quickly became my favorite pastime. Now, three daughters later, it's still one of my most loved hobbies!

In this book we've compiled more than 80 great layouts for you to duplicate or draw upon for inspiration. Whether you're creating pages for your children or friends, holidays or birthdays, you'll find dozens of great ideas. We've included chapters that show traditional layout techniques and digital scrapbooking, as well as chapters focusing on photos and creative ideas for journaling. If you're looking for unique ways to display your layouts, be sure to check out the chapter of projects that were designed with a bit of a twist on traditional scrapbooking applications.

I'm so excited to share this book with you, and I hope it becomes one of your favorite scrapbooking idea resources!

Warm regards,

Tanya

CONTENTS

EMPHASIS ON PHOTOS

6

Let your pictures speak for themselves. Capture an expression that says more than words, or a sunset that needs no description, and make it the focal point in your layout.

DIGITAL LAYOUTS

42

Software and digitally altered photos provide a fresh, new look for scrapbook pages.

BABIES & KIDS

64

Celebrate new arrivals and childhood milestones with creative and colorful layouts.

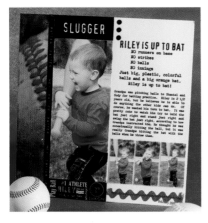

SPECIAL OCCASIONS
90

From weddings to a girls' night out, create stunning layouts to capture all the treasured moments in life.

JOURNALING
116

Discover creative and unique ways to add journaling to layouts with pockets, tags and more!

UNUSUAL SCRAPBOOK APPLICATIONS
140

Put a twist on traditional scrapbooking and create unique accent pieces to display in your home.

CHERISH

Spring

A thing of
beauty
is a
joy forever.

John Keats

PINK tulips

APRIL '06

CHERISH SPRING

DESIGN BY KATHLEEN PANEITZ

Close-up photos of brightly colored spring flowers are accented with a few carefully chosen embellishments.

Project note: Adhere paper, tag and photos with paper adhesive.

Center and adhere 7 x 5-inch photo to 9 x 7-inch piece of gingham printed paper; adhere to upper left corner of 12-inch square of card stock, ⅝ inch from top and left edges.

Adhere polka-dot tape down right side of layout, ⅛ inch from right edge of gingham paper; adhere another strip across layout ⅛ inch below bottom edge of gingham paper. Adhere plaid tape across layout ¼ inch below polka-dot tape.

Adhere tag to lower right corner of layout, ⅞ inch from right edge and ⅜ inch from bottom edge. Adhere 6 x 4-inch photo over tag, 1 inch from bottom edge of layout and ⅜ inch from right edge. Attach brad through hole in tag.

Adhere "A thing of beauty …" sticker in lower left corner of layout. Apply "Cherish" and flourish rub-on transfers over bottom edge of gingham printed paper in left corner. Adhere flourish rub-on transfers in upper right corner of layout; adhere alphabet rub-on transfers to spell "pink" and "tulips" to tag, overlapping top edge of photo. Apply rub-on transfers to spell month and year below lower left corner of smaller photo.

Apply rub-on transfers to spell "pring" to yellow card stock below plaid paper tape. Tie a double strand of pink floss around green chipboard "S"; using craft cement, adhere "S" to layout to form first letter in "Spring." ■

SOURCES: Printed paper and tag from Daisy D's Paper Co.; paper tape from Heidi Swapp; sticker from Cloud 9 Design; rub-on transfers from BasicGrey, Royal & Langnickel and Heidi Grace Designs; chipboard monogram from K&Company; brad from Karen Foster Design.

Materials

Color photo prints: 7 x 5 inches, 6 x 4 inches	½-inch-wide printed paper tape: pink/green plaid, white-on-pink mini polka dots	Rub-on transfers: black "Cherish," spring-themed words, alphabet, numerals, flourishes	⅝-inch round white brad
Pale yellow textured card stock	3½ x 6½-inch pink polka-dot tag	Pink floss or very fine raffia	Paper adhesive
Yellow-and-white gingham-check printed paper	"A thing of beauty …" transparent quotation sticker	2¾-inch chipboard "S" monogram	Craft cement

WONDER

DESIGN BY RACHAEL GIALLONGO

A candid shot, tightly cropped, is showcased in a simple digital layout.

Download and unzip digital scrapbooking and quotations kits. Open photo-editing program. Click "File," then "New" to create 12-inch-square canvas at 300 dpi.

Open photo file. Crop as desired, then size image to 9½ x 4 inches at 300 dpi.

Open folders containing the digital scrapbooking components. Use the Drag tool to layer printed papers, text and other elements as shown. Add journaling text.

Add drop shadows along bottom and right-hand edges of paper "layers" for the most realistic appearance.

Save file with JPEG extension at a quality of 10 for best printing results. Print layout onto glossy-finish photo paper. ■

SOURCES: Marsha Zepeda scrapbook kit and quote pack from www.TheDigiChick.com; Photoshop 7.0 from Adobe Systems Inc.

Materials

Digital photo	Digital scrapbooking kit	Computer with photo-editing software	Serif font of your choice
Wide-format glossy-finish photo paper	Digital quotations pack		Wide-format printer

ONLY THOSE WHO LOOK WITH THE EYES OF A CHILD CAN LOSE THEMSELVES IN THE OBJECT OF THEIR

w o n d e R

-EBERHARD ARNOLD

Dylan & Dane
April 2005

3 months old

Who is Redskins

Butterball
and his infamous game of "basket ambush".....

BUTTERBALL

DESIGN BY KATHLEEN PANEITZ

With a gleam in his eye, the ferocious Butterball plans his next attack. …

Project notes: If you have your photo enlarged at a photo store, ask how it will be trimmed. Many photo stores will print an 8 x 10-inch photo at 8 x 12 inches, and then trim it to 8 x 10 inches. If that is the case, request that your photo not be trimmed. Adhere card stock and photo with paper adhesive. Adhere other elements with craft cement.

Trim 1 inch off one edge of 12-inch-square sheet of tan card stock; center and adhere to 12-inch-square sheet of light beige card stock with left and right edges even.

Option: Use embossing tool on the reverse side of the photo to highlight some elements as desired.

Adhere photo to layout 2¾ inches from top edge with side edges even. Braid natural raffia to simulate basket handles; trim and adhere to layout, tucking ends of braided handles under edge of photo.

Adhere black alphabet stickers to tags to spell "Who," "is," "peek," and "ing." Tie stickers in order to raffia basket handles; adhere tags to layout.

Adhere white alphabet stickers across bottom of layout, over bottom edge of photo, to spell "Butterball." Write remaining caption on light beige card stock across bottom edge of layout using fine-tip pen.

Use computer to generate, or hand-print, puppy's age on white card stock to fit within bookplate. Trim card stock to size. Attach bookplate to layout near top edge, between raffia handles, using mini brads. Slide card stock into bookplate. ■

SOURCES: Alphabet stickers from Stickopotamus and Creative Imaginations; bookplate from Magic Scraps; computer font from Microsoft.

Materials

12 x 8-inch color photo print (see Project notes)	4 (1⅝ x 1⅛-inch) manila tags	2 brass mini brads	Printer (optional)
Card stock: light beige, tan, white	Alphabet stickers: black, white	Natural raffia	Paper glue
	Black fine-tip pen (optional)	Embossing tool (optional)	Craft cement
	3 x ¾-inch brass bookplate	Computer with Papyrus font (optional)	

ADMIRE

DESIGN BY TAMI MAYBERRY

A dramatic background accented by white zigzag stitching makes the black-and-white photo pop off the page.

Trim right edge of a 4 x 11-inch piece of red card stock in a wavy line; stamp red card stock randomly with circle patterns, stamping some images off edges of card stock. Adhere stamped red card stock to an 8½ x 11-inch piece of black card stock with top, bottom and left edges even.

Machine-stitch over wavy edge using white thread and zigzag stitch.

Adhere photo to white card stock; trim, leaving narrow borders. Adhere photo to layout ⅞ inch from top edge and ⁵⁄₁₆ inch from right edge.

Apply rub-on transfers to spell "Admire" along bottom edge of layout near lower right corner. ■

SOURCES: Stamps from Paper Salon; rub-on transfers from Paper House Productions.

Materials

6⅛ x 5⅞-inch black-and-white photo	Circle pattern stamps	White alphabet rub-on transfers to spell "admire"	Sewing machine with white thread
Card stock: white, black, red	Black ink pad		Paper adhesive

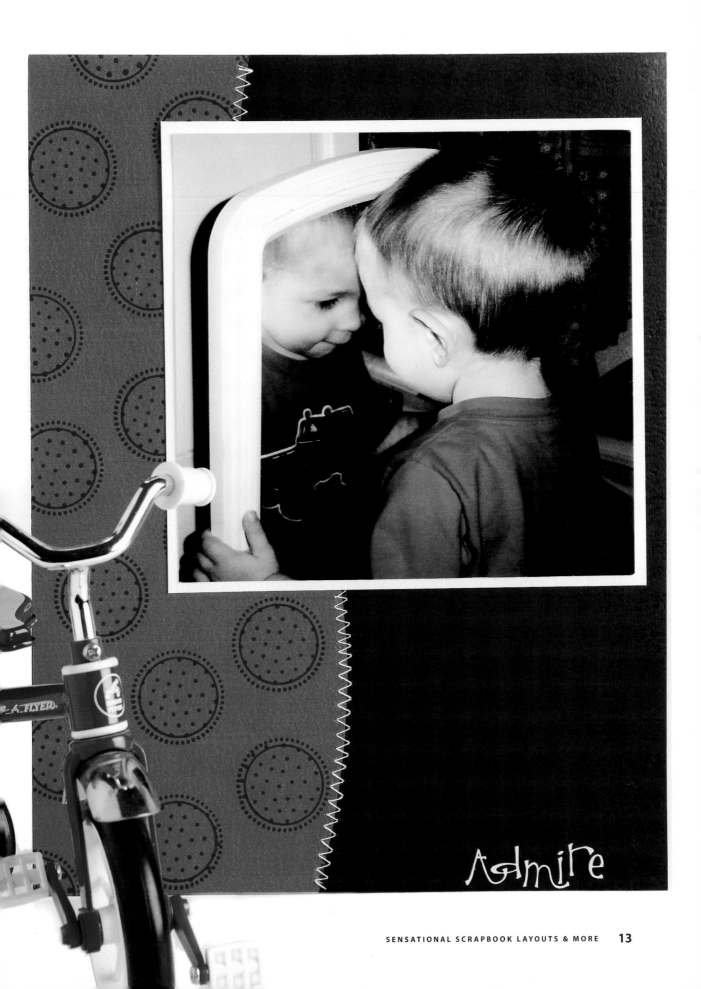

Admire

Materials

Color photo prints: 8½ x 8-inch, 4 (3½ x 5-inch)

Printed paper: blue, light blue, blue with white-stitched flowers, red with white-stitched flowers, yellow-green with white-stitched flowers, solid yellow-green, yellow-green/white floral, brick red/white stitching

Printable transparency

⅜-inch-wide royal blue ribbon with white polka-dot flowers

1¼-inch circle punch

Craft knife

Sewing machine with navy blue thread

Computer with fonts

Printer

Paper glue

Craft cement

A WARM SPRING DAY

DESIGN BY KRISTEN SWAIN

Die cuts, ribbons and machine stitching draw attention to darling portraits.

Project note: *Adhere paper and photos using paper glue; adhere ribbons using craft cement.*

Left page: Adhere a 3 x 12-inch strip of blue/white flowers printed paper to right edge of a 12-inch square of yellow-green paper with edges even. Adhere a 9 x 12-inch piece of yellow-green/white floral printed paper to remaining visible portion of yellow-green paper.

Adhere a 5-inch square of brick red/white stitching printed paper to layout 1¼ inches from left edge and ⅜ inch from top edge. Adhere a 5¾ x 3-inch piece of blue printed paper to layout ⅜ inch from right edge and ⁷⁄₁₆ inch from bottom edge.

Machine-stitch around yellow-green/white floral paper panel ⅛ inch from edge using navy blue thread and a short straight stitch; machine-stitch around brick red/white stitching square ⅛ inch from edge; stitch across bottom and top of blue rectangle ⅛ inch from edge.

Adhere photo to light blue printed paper; trim, leaving narrow borders. Adhere photo to layout ⅞ inch from top edge and 1½ inches from left edge.

Adhere ribbon across bottom of photo, near edge. Tie three 3-inch pieces of ribbon in knots; trim ends at an angle. Adhere one to ribbon on photo, 2 inches from left end. Adhere remaining ribbon knots to left edge of brick red/white stitching square.

Punch three circles with flowers from red/white-stitched

printed paper; adhere two over right edge of photo near bottom, and one barely overlapping left edge of blue panel.

Use computer to print "a warm" in reverse onto reverse side of solid red paper using a ½-inch font; print "spring" in reverse onto reverse side of light blue printed paper using a 1½-inch font. Cut out letters using a craft knife; adhere to blue panel as shown.

Right page: Adhere a 12 x 3-inch strip of blue/white-stitched printed paper across bottom of a 12-inch square of yellow-green/white-stitched printed paper with bottom and side edges even. Adhere a 7½-inch square of blue printed paper to yellow-green/white-stitched printed paper ¾ inch from top edge and 1⅛ inches from right edge.

Machine-stitch around blue paper panel ¼ inch from edges using a decorative stitch and navy blue thread. Use computer to generate journaling on transparency to fit within an area measuring 2 x 6¼ inches; trim transparency and adhere over right side of blue square. Adhere four 3½ x 5-inch color photos to layout as shown, leaving narrow margins between photos.

Punch three circles with flowers from red/white-stitched printed paper; adhere over edge of blue/white-stitched printed paper strip at bottom of layout. Knot a 3-inch piece of ribbon; trim ends at an angle. Adhere ribbon to lower right corner of stitched blue square as shown. ∎

SOURCE: Printed papers from Chatterbox; transparency from 3M.

The
cautious
seldom
err.

-Confucius

happiness

health

wealth

Dane! My sweet, cautious Dane! You are turning out to be just like me! You like to think things through and consider the risks. Some may call you fearful in your life, but I want you to know it's okay to take your time and be cautious. You don't need to be a risk taker. I believe that with your solid mind, you will find happiness, health & wealth!

Love always, Mom

HAPPINESS, HEALTH & WEALTH

DESIGN BY RACHAEL GIALLONGO

The photo's neutral background is the perfect place for a bold and graphic phrase.

Download and unzip digital scrapbooking kit. Open photo-editing program. Click "File," then "New" to create a 12-inch-square canvas at 300 dpi.

Open photo file. Crop photo as desired; then size to 10 x 7 inches at 300 dpi.

Open folders containing the digital scrapbooking components. Use the Drag tool to layer printed papers, text and other elements as shown. Add journaling text.

Add drop shadows along bottom and right-hand edges of paper "layers" for the most realistic appearance.

Save file with JPEG extension at a quality of 10 for best printing results. Print layout onto glossy-finish photo paper. ■

SOURCES: Heather Roselli scrapbook kit from www.TheDigiChick.com; Photoshop 7.0 from Adobe Systems Inc.

Materials

Digital photo	Digital scrapbooking kit	Serif font of your choice
Wide-format glossy-finish photo paper	Computer with photo-editing software	Wide-format printer

We may not
have it all
together, but
together we
have it all!

TOGETHER

DESIGN BY TAMI MAYBERRY

Match subtle background colors with printed paper to create an interesting, pulled-together look.

Center and adhere an 8¼ x 10¾-inch piece of black card stock to an 8½ x 11-inch piece of tan card stock. Adhere a 3 x 6¾-inch piece of printed paper to right side of layout, 1½ inches from top edge and right edges even.

Adhere ribbon across a 6¼ x 10-inch piece of red card stock, 1½ inches from bottom edge; trim ribbon even with edges of card stock. Attach paper clip over left end of ribbon and card stock.

Attach heart brad through right side of die-cut tag as shown; ink edges of tag with black ink pad. Adhere tag with brad to red card stock over ribbon ⅜ inch from right edge of red card stock. Adhere red card-stock panel to layout 3/16 inch from left edge of layout and ⅝ inch from top edge.

Adhere a 3¼ x 6½-inch piece of printed paper to upper left corner of red card stock panel, ⅛ inch from top and left edges.

Adhere photo to black card stock; trim, leaving narrow borders. Adhere photo to layout 2 inches from top edge and ⅛ inch from right edge. ■

SOURCES: Printed paper and die-cut tag from Three Bugs in a Rug; paper clip and heart brad from Creative Impressions.

Materials

7½ x 4⅝-inch color photo	Die-cut "we may not have	7/16-inch-wide tan grosgrain	7/16-inch red primitive-style
Card stock: black, tan, red	it all …" tag	ribbon	heart brad
Beige/burgundy/chocolate/	Black ink pad	Spiral black metal paper clip	Paper adhesive
celery polka-dot printed paper			

AN INSTANT OF LIFE

DESIGN BY EMILY DEISROTH

Frame a dramatic black-and-white photo with a selection of distressed papers.

Sand edges of photo and 12-inch square of card stock. *Note: Photo edges will turn red as pigment is sanded away.*

Cut a 12 x 3¾-inch strip from brown/bronze printed paper, trimming bottom edge just below "memory" quotation as shown; sand edges. Punch a 1-inch circle in lower right corner of strip. Adhere strip to card stock 3¼ inches from bottom edge.

Cut a 7 x 1¾-inch strip from orange/light gold printed paper; sand edges. Adhere strip to layout against top edge of first strip and even with right edge of card-stock page. Cut narrow slivers of green/teal/blue printed paper; adhere to card stock across top and bottom edges of printed paper strips.

Adhere photo to page at a slight angle, just above "memory" quotation. Cut circle of printed paper to fit inside photo turn; write year on circle using gel pen and adhere circle to photo turn. Attach photo turn to page at upper left corner of photo as shown.

Cut strips of words—"A photograph," "an instant of life," "captured for eternity," "looking back at you"—from card-stock quotations; ink edges using ink pad. Adhere "looking back at you" across circle punched in lower right corner of printed paper. Adhere "a photograph" to lower right corner of photo; adhere "an instant of life" and "captured for eternity" to bronze/light gold printed paper as shown. ∎

SOURCES: Card stock from BasicGrey, printed paper from 7gypsies and K&Company, die-cut quotes from KI Memories, photo turn from 7gypsies.

Materials

Black-and-white photo	quotation, Le Page orange/	Brown ink pad	1-inch circle punch
Jade "distressed" card stock	light gold texture print,	White gel pen	Paper adhesive
Printed papers: Left Bank Louvre	green/teal/blue print	Silver round photo turn	
brown/bronze with "memory"	Die-cut card-stock quotes	Fine sandpaper	

an instant of life

captured for eternity

A photograph Vibrates in

looking back at you

Ben & Nicholas Baer

COOL

Emily

May 2004

Okay, this is my all-time favorite picture of you, Em! How can I ever look at this big, funny smile and not be happy? This picture totally epitomizes your personality! Your shiny Tinkerbell shades and your shiny smile made for another happy day by the pool.

by the pool

COOL

DESIGN BY MELISSA SMITH

The happiest of summertime memories is recalled in this bright and sunny scrapbook page.

Project note: *Adhere elements using paper adhesive unless instructed otherwise.*

Adhere a 3⅞ x 8-inch piece of turtles paper to upper left corner of card stock with top and left edges even. Adhere 6 x 8-inch photo next to paper; adhere smaller photos next to larger photo. Adhere a 3⅞ x 4-inch piece of flip-flops paper to lower left corner of card stock with left and bottom edges even; adhere an 8⅛ x 4-inch piece of turtles paper to lower right corner.

Journaling: Use computer to print journaling onto transparency to fit over turtles paper in lower right corner; trim transparency to fit. Randomly press watermark ink onto edges of transparency; sprinkle ultra-thick embossing enamel over wet ink and heat with embossing gun to give the illusion of water drops. Adhere journaling to layout.

Name and date: Use computer to print name and date on transparency to fit over flip-flops paper in lower left corner; trim transparency to fit. Adhere to layout.

Adhere ¾-inch-wide strips cut from ribbon stripes paper over seams.

Using 11-point font, type three lines of "by the pool" (or other sentiment) repeatedly to fit across transparency, leaving at least five spaces above and below lines of text. Print onto transparency and cut into strips; center and adhere over ribbon strips. Attach orange brads at ends of vertical strip and green brads at ends of horizontal strip.

Title: Working within word-processing program, choose serif font and set size at 153 points; type "COOL." To print letters in reverse, choose "Print," then "Properties," then "Basics," then "Mirror Image." Feed ribbon stripes paper through printer to print letters on reverse side. Cut out letters using a craft knife. Adhere letters to card stock and cut out, leaving very narrow borders. Coat letters with thick gloss medium; adhere to turtles paper on left side of layout using foam tape.

Coat die cut with thick gloss medium. Poke hole through top with needle; thread 1-inch hanging loop of lime green floss through hole. Loop floss over "L" as shown; adhere flip-flops over intersection of ribbon strips using foam tape. ■

SOURCES: Printed paper and die cut from Anna Griffin Inc.; ink pad from Tsukineko; embossing enamel and gloss medium from Ranger Industries Inc.; brads from Making Memories; computer font and Word word-processing software from Microsoft.

Materials

Color photos: 6 x 8-inch, 2 (2³/₁₆ x 4-inch)	Printable transparency	Lime green floss	Adhesive foam tape
Green card stock	2½ x 2⅜-inch lime flip-flops die cut	Brads: 2 orange, 2 lime	Computer with serif font
Printed paper: orange/pink turtles, pink/lime flip-flops, pink/orange/lime ribbon stripes	Watermark ink pad	Craft knife	Printer
	Ultra-thick embossing enamel	Heat embossing gun	
	Thick gloss medium	Large needle	
		Paper adhesive	

GET WET

DESIGN BY LINDA BEESON

A larger-than-life photo and uncluttered background make a splash!

Edit and crop photo on computer, leaving room for text in upper left corner. ***Note:*** *Sample layout measures 8½ x 11 inches; photo is cropped to approximately 8¼ x 10¾ inches.* Use computer to generate "get wet" text on photo; print photo. ***Option:*** *Add text to printed photo using rub-on transfers or alphabet stickers.* Center and adhere photo to 8½ x 11-inch piece of red card stock.

Use computer to generate text and journaling, printing it in red on lower right corner of a piece of orange card stock. Trim printed card stock to 8¼ x 2¾ inches; trim wave along top edge. Trim complementary wavy edges along tops of an 8¼ x 2¹³⁄₁₆-inch strip of red card stock and an 8¼ x 3-inch strip of white card stock. Layer strips, side and bottom edges even; adhere to each other and to bottom of photo.

Use computer to generate child's name printed repeatedly around a 1¼-inch circle; reverse color so that background is colored. Print in red onto orange card stock. Punch or cut a 1⅜-inch circle around lettering. Center and adhere circle to a 1½-inch circle punched or cut from orange card stock; center and adhere circles to a 1¾-inch circle punched or cut from red card stock. Adhere over edges of wavy strips as shown in photo. ■

Materials

Digital photo or photo print of desired size

Matte-finish photo paper (optional)

Card stock: red, orange, white

Circle punches or templates: 1¾-inch, 1½-inch, 1⅜-inch

Computer with photo-editing software (optional)

Computer font, alphabet rub-on transfers, or alphabet stickers

Color printer (optional)

Paper adhesive

get
wet

stay cool
make a splash
waterlogged
swimming lessons - 2004

ONE FINE DAY

DESIGN BY EMILY DEISROTH

Multiple photos and minimal use of embellishments create an attractive layout of a special occasion.

Project note: Adhere photos and paper using paper adhesive. Adhere remaining elements using craft cement.

Crop photos as desired. Call attention to the main photo with a narrow white border. Ink edges of remaining photos using brown ink pad.

Arrange photos on beige card stock as desired, positioning most of the photo layout within two-thirds of the page. *Note: Sample layout measures 12 inches square.* Using circle punch, punch a half-circle over lower right edge of top photo in layout. Adhere photos to beige card stock. Adhere square epoxy tile over photo corners where they meet in center.

Tear a piece of polka-dot printed paper to accent main photo; adhere to page below photo's lower right corner. Trim ribbon to same width as main photo; adhere across bottom edge of photo.

Using rub-on transfers, add lettering and image to page as desired. Punch holes through page and ribbon using paper piercer or awl; mount word brad through holes, wrapping twist tie around word brad attached through ribbon.

Adhere glass pebbles to edges of page as shown. ■

SOURCES: Printed paper from Chatterbox; rub-on transfers from Making Memories and 7gypsies; ribbon from American Crafts; word brad from K&Company; twist tie from Pebbles.

Materials

4 x 6-inch color photos	Dark brown ink pad	½-inch-wide green-and-white–striped grosgrain ribbon	Glass craft pebbles
Card stock: white (optional), beige textured	Rub-on transfers: black, green and white alphabets; white kite motif	Printed twist tie	1-inch circle punch
Brown/cream polka-dot printed paper		2 word brads	Paper piercer or awl
		$5/8$-inch-square epoxy tile	Paper adhesive
			Craft cement

It was one fine day

out together

f beautieS which I try to catch as they fly by, for who knows whether any of them will ever return? M
Anyone who keeps the ability to see beauty never grows old·Franz Kafka   Exhaust the little moment·Soon it
And be it cash or gold·   will not come

Beyond Magic

BEYOND MAGIC

DESIGN BY EMILY DEISROTH

A change of elevation creates a dramatic point of view in any photograph.

Project note: Adhere photo and paper using paper adhesive. Adhere remaining elements using craft cement.

Print and crop photo so that its width matches card stock and length is equal to roughly two-thirds of card stock's length. *Note: On sample layout, card stock is 12 inches square; cropped photo measures 12 x 7½ inches.*

Punch a 1-inch circle through card stock near lower right corner. Punch circular "bites" across remaining bottom edge of card stock as shown in photo. Ink edges of punched circle and "bites" using ink pad.

Cut a 12 x 1-inch strip from printed paper, choosing a section with appropriate words for your photo in bottom ½ inch of strip. Adhere strip to reverse side of photo along bottom edge, leaving ½ inch of strip visible from front. Ink bottom edge of printed paper strip using ink pad. Adhere photo and printed paper strip to card stock with top and side edges even.

Cut another 12-inch-wide strip of printed paper tall enough to fill in punched circle and "bites" along bottom of card stock; adhere to reverse side of card stock with bottom edges even.

Adhere a 12-inch strip of black stitched ribbon across card stock 1½ inches from bottom edge of photo. Fray ½ inch at each end of a 13-inch piece of striped ribbon; center and adhere to card stock directly below black stitched ribbon. Apply "beyond magic" rub-on transfer to striped ribbon near right edge of layout using rub-on transfers.

Adhere typewriter key to center of photo turn; let dry. Attach green brad through hole in photo turn; adhere photo turn in center of punched circle using craft cement. Add journaling around edges of circular "bites" using fine-tip pen. Ink edges of entire layout, including photo, using ink pad. ■

SOURCES: Printed paper, typewriter key and photo turn from 7gypsies; rub-on transfers from Making Memories; ribbons from Making Memories and Li'l Davis Designs.

Materials

Photo print, sized to fit on layout	Fine-tip black marker	Grosgrain ribbon: ³/₁₆-inch-wide black with white stitching,	Typewriter key embellishment
White card stock	Black alphabet rub-on transfers	⁷/₈-inch-wide green-and-	1-inch circle punch
"Typed" printed paper	Green mini brad	white stripe	Paper adhesive
Black ink pad		Silver round photo turn	Craft cement

IN THE BLINK OF AN EYE

DESIGN BY RACHAEL GIALLONGO

Bold, bright colors and a graphic photo draw the eye into this layout.

Download and unzip digital scrapbooking and embellishment kits. Open photo-editing program. Click "File," then "New" to create a 12-inch-square canvas at 300 dpi.

Open photo. Crop as desired, then size photo to 6½ x 7½ inches at 300 dpi.

Open folders containing the digital scrapbooking components. Use the Drag tool to layer printed papers, text and other elements as shown. Add journaling text. Add drop shadows along edges of paper "layers" for the most realistic appearance.

Save file with JPEG extension at a quality of 10 for best printing results. Print layout onto glossy-finish photo paper. ■

SOURCES: Kathy Moore scrapbook kit from www.ACherryOnTop.com; Dani Mogstad digital glass bauble from www.DesignbyDani.com, Photoshop 7.0 from Adobe Systems Inc., computer fonts from www.CreatingKeepsakes.com

Materials

Digital photo	Digital scrapbooking kit	Computer with photo-editing	Computer fonts: CK Bella,
Wide-format glossy-finish	Digital glass bauble	software	CK Constitution
photo paper	embellishment		Wide-format printer

in the blink
of an
eye

Scott,

It seems like just yesterday you took this picture. Megan had eyed these adorable doll beds and being the woodcrafter that you are, you snapped this photo with plans to build her one just like them. But, you blinked.

That's all it took- the blink of an eye. Two years passed and visions of doll beds with colorful blankets have been replaced with talk of boys, laptops and cell phones.

Pay attention, honey... if you blink again, the talk may be of caterers, dj's and honey moon plans.

Love,

Rachael

Materials

Digital photo

Card stock: taupe, orange, aqua, dark blue

Orange/aqua/blue/taupe printed paper: surfboard, circles, floral, alphabet

Glossy photo paper

Blue chalk ink

Blue felt-tip marker

3 large blue rhinestone brads

⅝-inch-wide ribbon: aqua, orange/white stripe

Blue rickrack

Circle punches: 1¼-inch, 1½-inch

Hole punches: ¹⁄₁₆-inch, ³⁄₁₆-inch

1-inch flower die-cutter

Label maker with blue tape

Computer with photo-editing software

Old Type font

Printer

SURFER BOI

DESIGN BY LYNNE WILSON

Digital lettering is an ideal way to frame your little surfer catching a wave.

Create a digital brush: Working within photo-editing program, create a new document of desired size. Click on Ellipse tool; select Type in Path tool (square with pen in the center) from toolbar at top; create circle.

Select Text tool; click on circle where you want title to be. Type title. To place your title inside the circle rather than outside, highlight the title; select "Edit," then "Transform Path," then "Flip Vertical." Adjust font size and spacing as desired, leaving spaces between words or phrases for attaching embellishments later. Save image as a JPEG file.

Close working file; open the JPEG file you just created. Select "Edit," then "Define Brush Preset." Name the brush when prompted to do so. ***Note:*** *This digital brush works like a stamp. You can adjust the size, color and opacity of the "stamped" image as desired.*

Photo: Begin with black-and-white digital photo measuring approximately 11½ x 7 inches. Select Brush tool; on top toolbar, select the digital brush you just created from the list of specific brushes (it will appear last on the list).

Resize the brush as desired and choose its color. Click brush or "stamp" image onto photo. Save photo and print. Punch half of a 1½-inch circle along lower right edge of photo, near bottom.

Layout: Center and adhere photo to 12-inch-square of taupe card stock near top edge. Using felt-tip marker, write date on 1¼-inch circle punched from aqua card stock. Ink edges of circle and adhere inside cutout on right edge of photo, allowing circle to protrude off edge of page.

Cut a 12 x ½-inch strip from each of three printed papers; ink edges. Punch ⅛-inch and ⅜-inch holes through some circles in circles strip. Knot ribbons and rickrack around another strip near right end. Referring to photo, adhere strips across layout in a fairly random fashion, positioning strip with ribbons and rickrack in middle.

Punch 1¼-inch and 1½-inch circles from printed papers and aqua, dark blue and orange card stocks. Punch 1¼-inch circles from the centers of some 1½-inch circles to create rings; ink edges of circles and rings. Adhere circles and rings in a slightly wavy overlapping row across layout under photo.

Die-cut three flowers from orange card stock; ink edges and attach to photo in spaces within circular title using rhinestone brads. Using surfboard motif from printed paper as a template, cut three surfboards from assorted printed papers; ink edges and adhere, overlapping edges, to lower right corner of photo. Print subtitle on blue label tape; affix to photo over surfboards. ∎

SOURCES: Printed paper from Arctic Frog; die cutter from QuicKutz Inc.; chalk ink from Clearsnap Inc.; brads from Making Memories; ribbons from May Arts; label maker from DYMO Corp.; hole punch from Fiskars; circle punches from EK Success Ltd.; Photoshop CS2 from Adobe Systems Inc.; font from 2 Peas in a Bucket Inc.

CUTE AS A BUTTON

DESIGN BY LYNNE WILSON

They say a picture is worth a thousand words,
and this button-framed photo is no exception.

Center and adhere photo to 12-inch square of brown card stock near top edge. Using glossy adhesive, adhere several clear buttons of assorted sizes to right side of printed paper; when dry, trim around buttons. Adhere paper-backed buttons and other buttons around edges of photo using adhesive dots.

Thread a 13-inch piece of each ribbon through buckle. Adhere ribbons across bottom of layout as shown, grouping them closer together on the left side and farther apart on right side, and positioning buckle 3½ inches from left edge of layout. Adhere ribbon ends to reverse side of layout; staple ribbon ends from front to secure. Tie mini pompom trim around buckle as shown. ■

SOURCES: Printed paper from Scrapworks Inc.; clear buttons from Foofala; ribbons from Scrapworks and May Arts; pompom trim from May Arts; adhesive dots from Glue Dots International; glossy adhesive from KI Gloo.

Materials

10 x 8-inch color photo	Buttons: ½- to ⅞-inch clear	⁷⁄₁₆-inch-wide printed grosgrain	1½-inch white pearl buckle
Brown card stock	buttons, complementary	ribbons: green/yellow daisies,	Stapler with staples
Green/pink/magenta striped	buttons in assorted colors	brown/white dots, pink/	Paper adhesive
printed paper	and sizes	magenta circles	Adhesive dots
		White mini pompom trim	Clear glossy adhesive

Princess Party

12 little girls
12 princess costumes
1 loud tea party
1 fantastic day

PRINCESS PARTY

DESIGN BY LYNNE WILSON

A bright, colorful photo and basic journaling combine for a great layout design for scrapbooking your next themed party.

Working in photo-editing program, size main photo to approximately 5 x 11 inches; print. Lay photo on 12-inch square of white card stock to determine best position for title. On computer, set page size to 12 inches square. Print title and journaling directly onto white card-stock background, using purple ink for title and black ink for journaling, and omitting first letter in each word, as they will be replaced by stencil letters.

Adhere photo to yellow card stock and trim, leaving narrow borders. Adhere photo to layout just above title.

Use rubber letter stencil to add first letter of title words: Adhere wide double-sided tape across reverse side of stencil, covering cutout letter; pour microbeads into letter and onto tape and press to adhere firmly. Staple three pieces of ribbon to left edge of stencil; press stencil onto layout at beginning of title, overlapping photo slightly as shown. Adhere letter punched from stencil to beginning of second word in title.

Cut a V-shaped notch in the right edge of a 1 x 11-inch strip of striped paper; adhere strip to lower section of layout as shown, aligning it with left edge.

Size three remaining photos to 2 inches square; print. Adhere photos in a vertical row along right side of layout over printed paper strip. ∎

SOURCES: Printed paper and rubber letter stencil from Scrapworks Inc.; ribbons and rickrack from May Arts; adhesive tape from Magic Scraps; fonts from www.dafont.com and www.momscorner4kids.com; printer from Canon.

Materials

4 digital photos	Rubber letter stencil	Stapler with staples	Computer fonts: Eight Track,
Card stock: white, yellow	Microbeads	Wide adhesive tape	Susie's Hand
Striped printed paper	Coordinating ribbons:	Computer with photo-editing	Wide-format printer
Photo paper	sheer, dotted	software	
	Purple rickrack		

A FATHER'S LOVE

DESIGN BY SUSAN STRINGFELLOW

The title, created in an elegant font, reflects the emotion on the faces in the photo featured in this layout.

Project note: Adhere elements using paper adhesive unless instructed otherwise.

Center and adhere an 11½-inch square of light green paper to 12-inch square of green card stock. Adhere an 11 x 2½-inch strip of green striped paper across layout near bottom edge. Adhere a 4¾-inch square of pink paper to lower left corner of layout as shown. Cut individual flourishes from green flourishes paper and adhere to left side of layout and upper left corner; adhere half-pearls and rhinestones to flourishes using craft glue.

Apply "moment" phrase rub-on transfer to lower left corner of layout. Apply a flourish rub-on transfer below phrase.

Adhere photo to white card stock and trim, leaving ⅛-inch borders. Attach photo corners; adhere photo to layout as shown.

Lay three 10-inch strips of piping side by side; machine-stitch across one end. Braid piping strips; temporarily adhere loose ends to lower right corner

of layout, 1 inch from bottom edge. Lay three 6-inch lengths of piping side by side; machine-stitch across one end. Braid piping strips; temporarily adhere loose ends to lower left corner of layout 1 inch from bottom edge, in line with first braid. Thread braids through buckle 1½ inches from left edge of photo. Adhere braid and buckle to layout using craft glue.

Machine-stitch around edge of green paper using a straight stitch and white thread and stitching over loose ends of braided piping. Machine-stitch across bottom edge of striped paper.

Apply alphabet rub-on transfers to spell "A father's LOVE" up left edge of layout, adding flourish rub-on transfer to ends. Apply rub-on transfers for date to lower right corner of layout on striped paper; apply a flourish rub-on transfer at each end. ■

SOURCES: Printed papers, rhinestones and buckle from K&Company; rub-on transfers from Delish and BasicGrey; half-pearls from Making Memories.

Materials

8 x 10-inch color photo	Black rub-on transfers: alphabet	White satin piping	Paper adhesive
Card stock: green, white	letters, "moment" phrase,	1-inch gold antique-style buckle	Craft glue
Printed paper: light green, green	flourishes	Craft knife	
striped, pink, green flourishes	Half-pearls	Sewing machine and	
4 black photo corners	Small gold rhinestones	white thread	

A father's LOVE

A Single MOMENT IN TIME

July 2006

CELEBRATE

DESIGN BY SUSAN STRINGFELLOW

Brightly colored fabric flowers are the perfect way to enhance a photo from your big day.

Center and adhere an 11½-inch square of striped paper to a 12-inch square of black card stock with stripes running vertically. Adhere a 10½-inch square of white card stock to striped paper ⅜ inch from top, ⅝ inch from bottom and centered from side to side. Adhere an 8½ x ⅛-inch strip of paisley paper across bottom of layout 1¼ inches from bottom edge of layout and right edges even.

Machine-stitch around layout over edges of white card stock using black thread and a zigzag stitch.

Adhere photo to white card stock ⁵⁄₁₆ inch from top edge of white card stock.

Print "celebrate!" in a 1⅛-inch font in reverse on black card stock; cut out letters with craft knife and adhere to layout over paisley strip.

Flower border: Adhere premade red and yellow flowers along bottom edge of photo as shown. Attach purple flowers with rhinestone brads. Punch three ⅝-inch flowers from turquoise/lime sections of striped paper; center each on a coral flower. Attach coral flowers and paper flower centers with black mini brads. Fold five 2-inch squares of black netting accordion-style; adhere one end of each under edges of flowers, fanning out netting as shown.

Add names or other journaling to striped card-stock border in lower right corner using fine-tip black pen. ■

SOURCES: Printed paper from My Mind's Eye; pen from Faber-Castell; premade flowers from Creative Co-op Inc.; silk flowers from Teters; rhinestone brads and mini brads from Making Memories; flower punch from EK Success Ltd.

Materials

- 10 x 8-inch color photo
- Black card stock
- Lime/turquoise/pink printed papers: stripes, paisley print
- Fine-tip black marker

- Premade silk flowers with centers: 2½-inch red, 2 (1⅝-inch) yellow
- Silk flowers: 2 (1¾-inch) purple, 1½-inch purple, 3 (1½-inch) coral

- 3 rhinestone brads
- 3 black mini brads
- Black netting
- ½-inch flower punch
- Craft knife

- Sewing machine with black thread
- Paper adhesive
- Computer with printer

celebrate!

Clarissa and Jimmy

3-IN-1

DESIGNS BY TAMI MAYBERRY

A little digital manipulation is all that's needed to enhance less-than-perfect photos.

Even on a good photo, the colors sometimes do not go well together. A good example is the red and pink clothing the girls are wearing in the photo in the first layout, "Sister, I Love You." This is a problem that can make designing with photos difficult. By desaturating the color in the photo, as in the second layout, "Love," the colors coordinate better and are easier to work with. If the colors clash severely or simply have the wrong "feel" for the layout, converting the photo to black-and-white as in the third layout, "Priceless," will give the layout a more dramatic look.

Sister, I Love You

Project note: Adhere photo and paper using paper adhesive. Adhere other elements using craft cement.

Adhere a 6 x 10¾-inch piece of circles printed paper to an 8½ x 11-inch piece of black card stock ¼ inch from top, left and bottom edges. Adhere a 6 x 8-inch piece of floral printed paper to layout ¼ inch from right edge and 1 inch from top edge.

Adhere photo to black card stock; trim, leaving ⅛-inch borders. Adhere photo to layout ¾ inch from left edge and 1¼ inches from top edge.

Adhere a 7-inch piece of ribbon across layout 1½ inches from bottom edge, wrapping left end over left edge and securing it on reverse side of layout. Adhere daisies together in layers; adhere bottle cap in center. Adhere daisies in lower right corner of layout, over right end of ribbon.

Adhere "I love you" tag to layout in upper right corner as shown; adhere metal tile in cutout opening in tag. ■

SOURCES: Printed paper from Carolee's Creations and Scrapworks; metal tile from Making Memories; plastic tag from Pebbles Inc.; bottle cap from Li'l Davis Designs; ribbon from Creative Impressions.

Materials

5¼ x 7-inch color photo	"Sister" metal word tile	5⁄16-inch-wide sheer black ribbon	Paper adhesive
Black card stock	"I love you" plastic tag	3 (3-inch) pink silk daisies	Craft cement
Printed paper: red-on-pink circles, pink floral print	"Love and cherish" bottle cap	Printer	

Love

Project note: Adhere photo, card stock and paper using paper adhesive. Adhere other elements using craft cement.

Photo: Desaturate color as desired using photo-editing software. Size to 5 x 7 inches and print; trim.

Layout: Center and adhere a 7½ x 10¾-inch piece of brown card stock to an 8½ x 11-inch piece of cream card stock. Round off upper right and lower right corners of a 7½ x 8¼-inch piece of printed paper; adhere paper to layout ½ inch from top edge and with left edges even.

Adhere photo to pink card stock; trim, leaving ³⁄₁₆-inch borders. Adhere matted photo to pale pink card stock; trim, leaving ³⁄₁₆-inch borders. Adhere "my sister, my friend" rub-on transfer to bottom portion of photo. Adhere fabric tag to reverse side of matted photo, near upper right corner. Center and adhere photo to pink printed paper on layout.

Adhere fabric alphabet stickers to spell "love" in lower right corner of layout as shown; adhere flower rub-on transfer to brown card stock slightly to left of "love" stickers. Adhere an 8¼-inch strip of rickrack down left edge of pink printed paper, ⅜ inch from left edge of layout. ■

SOURCES: Printed paper from Blue Cardigan Designs; rub-on transfers, fabric alphabet stickers and fabric tab from Scrapworks.

Materials

Digital photo	Rub-on transfers: "my sister, my friend," flower	Brown rickrack	Paper adhesive
Glossy-finish photo paper		Corner rounder punch	Craft cement
Card stock: brown, cream, pink, pale pink	Pink fabric alphabet stickers to spell "love"	Computer with photo-editing software	
Pink-on-pink printed paper	"Cherish" fabric tab	Printer	

Priceless

Photo: Transform photo to black-and-white using photo-editing software. Size to 4⅜ x 6 inches and print; trim.

Layout: Punch two flowers from rust card stock and one flower from teal card stock. Die-cut circle frame from teal card stock. Add dots and details to flowers and frame using felt-tip marker.

Adhere circular frame in upper left corner of an 8½ x 11-inch piece of olive card stock ½ inch from top and left edges. Adhere rust punched flower inside frame, positioning it slightly toward top and left.

Adhere a 6¼ x 7½-inch piece of teal card stock to olive card stock 1¼ inches from left edge and 1⅛ inches from top edge. Adhere photo to rust card stock; trim, leaving narrow border. Center and adhere photo to teal card stock on layout ⁵⁄₁₆ inch from top edge of teal card stock.

Apply "priceless" rub-on transfer to olive card stock below teal panel as shown in photo. Adhere teal flower to right of rub-on transfer; adhere remaining rust flower to teal card stock below photo. Add details and dots to layout as desired using felt-tip marker. ■

SOURCES: Rub-on transfer from All My Memories; flower punch from Family Treasures.

Materials

Digital photo	"priceless" rub-on transfer	Die-cutting machine with 2-inch circular frame die	Printer
Glossy-finish photo paper	Black felt-tip marker	Computer with photo-editing software	Paper adhesive
Card stock: olive, teal, rust	1-inch flower punch		

Katie's Famous Face

affectionately
nicknamed,
"the Face"
by Mrs. t.
04

KATIE'S FAMOUS FACE

DESIGN BY STEPHANIE BARNARD

A bit of bold color highlights the focal point of this digital layout.

Open digital photo on computer; convert image to black-and-white, and then enhance with color as desired using digital imaging software. Crop as desired. ***Note:*** *Sample layout measures 12 inches square.* Use computer to generate text and journaling on photo. Save file. ***Option:***

Tint enlarged, cropped photo using photo-tinting markers. Add text using rub-on transfers.

Print photo and text onto photo paper using wide-format printer. ***Option:*** *Have photo printed at photo shop.* ∎

Materials

Digital photo or photo print of desired size

Wide-format photo paper

Photo-tinting markers (optional)

Computer with digital imaging software (optional)

Computer font or alphabet rub-on transfers

Wide-format printer (optional)

GIRLS' NIGHT OUT

DESIGN BY MANDY KOONTZ

A milestone birthday celebration with friends is remembered in this digital layout.

Open a new document within photo-editing program; set up document as follows: size: 8 inches square; resolution: 300 px; RGB color mode; transparent background content. Click "OK."

Open digital scrapbooking kit; open "MCO_Kraft Paper" file. Use Move tool to click and drag file to new document. Open file containing "All American" kit elements; open "NRJ_AA_Swirl_Over" file. Use Move tool to click and drag file to overlay kraft paper. Center overlay with swirls positioned in lower right and upper left corners.

Open photo; click and drag onto background. *Note: If photo is behind kraft paper background, press ctrl +] until photo is visible on top layer. To add white border around photo, right-click on photo's layer in Layer palette; then click "Blending Options." Click on "Stroke"; set stroke size at 30, position to inside, blend mode to normal, opacity to 100 percent, and fill type to color; use color picker to change color from red to white. Click "OK"; then, in left-hand column, click on "Drop Shadow" to add drop shadow; click "OK."*

Open file containing glitter flower, then "Glitter Flower 4" file. Using Move tool, click and drag flower to lower right corner of photo; add a drop shadow.

Open kit containing tags; open "tag1" and "tag4" files. Using Move tool, click and drag tag 1 to layout, placing it on top of glitter flower. Use ctrl + [to move tag layer behind flower layer. Click "Edit," then "Transform," then "Rotate," and rotate tag slightly in counterclockwise direction. Click Move tool, then "Apply"; or click checkmark in toolbar at top of workspace to accept changes made to the tag. Add drop shadow.

Click and drag tag 4 to layout, arranging layer so that it rests behind glitter flower but on top of first tag. Add a drop shadow.

Year: Choose Text tool from toolbar; set foreground color to black in color picker. Choose 30-point font; click on tag, type text, then click on checkmark at top of workspace to accept.

Circle a subject in photo: Choose Elliptical Marquee tool from photo-editing program's toolbox; use mouse to click and drag around desired subject, leaving a selection of "marching ants." Add a new layer by going to "Layer," then "New," then "Layer"; click "OK." Click on "Edit," then "Stroke." Set width at 15–20 px, color to white, location to outside, mode to normal, opacity to 100 percent and leave preserve transparency unchecked. Click "OK."

Using Text tool and desired font, add black text below photo and in upper left corner of layout, leaving room at left for title. Working in tablet doodles program, add arrows, smiley faces and underlines to layout as desired.

Title: Using Text tool, set foreground to black in color picker. Using desired font, type "OUT" at about 225 points; click arrow at top of workspace to accept. Using desired font, type "Girls Night" in same color as glitter flower by using color picker to draw color out. Click checkmark at top to accept. Rotate text by clicking "Edit," then "Transform," then "Rotate," and rotate text in counterclockwise direction. Click checkmark at top to accept. Print layout. ∎

SOURCES: Digital kraft paper and swirl overlay from All American digital scrapbooking kit by Michelle Coleman and Nancy Rowe Janitz; glitter flower from Holly McCaig; tags from Priceless Goods digital kit by Jen Wilson; tablet doodles from Wacom; Photoshop digital imaging software from Adobe Systems Inc.

Peggy left the waiter a funny tip"

OUT

Girls Night

We met for dinner at a little mexican restaurant for Lara's 21st birthday

2006

Materials

Black-and-white digital photo	Digital swirl overlay	Digital tablet doodles	Printer
Photo paper	Digital glitter flower	Computer with photo-editing	
Digital kraft paper	Digital tags	software	

SAVVY

DESIGN BY SUSAN STRINGFELLOW

A large, dramatic photo is the centerpiece of a muted, low-key layout.

Project note: *Adhere paper and photos with paper adhesive. Adhere remaining elements with craft cement.*

Photo: Open photo within photo-editing program; choose "Layer," then select "Duplicate Layer." Go to "Image," then "Duplicate," and create duplicate to open a new copy of your photo image. Change duplicate layer to black-and-white image by going to "Image," then "Adjustments," then "Desaturate."

Select Eraser tool. Zoom image size to 100 percent, and use tool to erase areas where you wish to reveal color. When you are satisfied with the image, select "Layer," then "Flatten Image." Save image and print. *Note: On sample project, photo is printed to 8⅜ x 7 inches, including ¼-inch white borders; complete layout measures 12 inches square.*

Layout: Round corners on a 3½ x 11½-inch strip of gray printed paper. Center and adhere strip to 12-inch square of light gray printed card stock ½ inch from left edge. Adhere a 6½ x 1¼-inch strip of paisley printed paper to bottom left corner of layout, with bottom and left edges even with edges of card stock.

Referring to photo throughout, draw a wavy, narrow, free-form square border with swirls in lower left corner on back of black printed paper; border should measure about 11½ inches square. Cut out using craft knife; turn over, center and adhere border to layout.

Round off upper left and lower left corners on a 10 x 8-inch piece of black printed paper; adhere near upper right corner of layout, inside black free-form border, with edges ⅝ inch from top edge of layout and ½ inch from right edge of layout. Adhere an 8¾ x 7½-inch piece of teal printed paper toward upper right corner of black printed paper, ⅛ inch from top and right edges. Adhere photo to teal paper ⅛ inch from top and right edges.

Using fine-tip marker, write descriptive words or names on teal paper margins along left and bottom edges of photo. Write a couple of words on scraps of teal printed paper; cut out, sand edges, and adhere to border of handwritten words. Write age or date directly onto card stock in margin to right of photo.

Sand edges of a 5 x ¼-inch strip of teal printed paper; adhere over top edge of paisley strip in bottom left corner of layout, with left end of teal strip even with left edge of layout. Ink edges of layout with black ink pad.

Adhere 3-inch strips of brocade ribbon and rickrack near upper left corner of layout, 1¾ inches from top edge; trim even with edge of layout.

Machine-stitch in a wavy line over and around black free-form border using black thread and a short, straight stitch. Machine-stitch around edge of black printed paper under photo, using white thread and a combination of straight and zigzag stitches.

Apply alphabet stickers vertically to lower left area of layout to spell "irresistible." Using black paint as ink, stamp "SAVVY" across bottom of layout using 2-inch alphabet stamps. Using teal paint as ink, stamp a question mark at end of word. When paint is dry, stamp over black letters using swirl/vine stamp and teal paint.

Adhere paisley printed paper to chipboard scrap; cut out 1⅛-inch primitive-style heart. Sand edges; set eyelet in heart. Link jump rings; attach one end to heart through eyelet and other end to safety pin. Pin heart to brocade ribbon and rickrack. Tie a 2½-inch piece of white ribbon to safety pin, allowing ends to fray.

SOURCES: Card stock, printed paper, stickers and ribbon from BasicGrey; rubber stamps from Sugarloaf Products; eyelet from Eyelet Outlet.

Materials

Digital photo

Glossy-finish photo paper

Light gray printed card stock

Printed paper: gray print, blue-and-green paisley, solid black, black print, teal print

Chipboard scrap

½-inch alphabet stickers to spell "irresistible"

Stamps: 2-inch alphabet and question mark, decorative swirl/vine

Acrylic paint: black, teal

Black ink pad

Black fine-tip marker

Ribbon: ¾-inch-wide black/silver/white brocade, 3/16-inch-wide white crochet style

Black velvet rickrack

3 silver jump rings

Small black safety pin

Teal eyelet

Corner rounder punch

Craft knife

Sewing machine

Sewing thread: black, white

Eyelet-setting tool

Fine sandpaper

Jewelry pliers

Computer with photo-editing software

Color printer

Paper adhesive

Craft cement

a daughter is a miracle that never ceases to be miraculous...
full of beauty and forever beautiful
...loving and caring and truly amazing.
—deanna beisser

sweet

SWEET

DESIGN BY TAMI MAYBERRY

Careful photo placement creates a dramatic composition that draws the eye to the center of the layout.

Project note: Adhere photos and paper using paper adhesive. Adhere other elements using craft glue.

Background photo: Open photo image within photo-editing software. Click on "Enhance" option in main toolbar; select "Adjust Lighting" and click on "Brightness/Contrast." Increase brightness level and decrease contrast level. Click "OK."

Select Text option in tool palette. Choose font and text size. Click on photo to position text; type in desired text. Save and print. *Note: On sample layout, this photo measures 6¼ x 8½ inches; complete layout measures 11 x 8½ inches.*

Layout: Adhere background photo to left side of 11 x 8½-inch piece of white card stock. Adhere a 4¾ x 8½-inch piece of printed paper to right side of card stock. Adhere ribbon over seam between papers.

Adhere 4¼ x 6¼-inch photo to pink card stock; trim, leaving narrow borders. Adhere photo to layout ¾ inch from top edge and 1½ inches from right edge. Attach photo turns over upper right edge of photo using mini brads.

Layer pink flowers and adhere to layout over lower right corner of photo. Adhere sticker to flowers' center; adhere concho to frame sticker. ∎

SOURCES: Printed paper from American Traditional Designs; sticker and concho from Scrapworks; photo turn mounts and ribbon from Creative Impressions; Photoshop Elements from Adobe Systems Inc.

Materials

Digital photo, 4¼ x 6¼-inch color print of same photo	White-on-pink polka-dot printed paper	1-inch round pink concho	Computer with photo-editing software
Glossy-finish photo paper	1-inch round pink "sweet" sticker	¼-inch-wide pink-and-white gingham-check ribbon	Printer
Card stock: pink, white	2 white photo turn mounts	2 (3-inch) pink silk daisies	Paper adhesive
	2 white mini brads		Craft glue

FALL LEAVES

DESIGN BY SHERRY WRIGHT

Playful use of color in a digitally manipulated photo is enhanced by playful embellishments.

Photo: Open photo within photo-editing program. Click on "Layer," then "New layer via copy." Convert new layer to black-and-white by clicking on "Enhance," then "Adjust color, hue/saturation." Move "Saturation" bar all the way to the left; click "OK."

Choose Eraser tool from tool palette. Erase areas of black-and-white photo in which you want color to be visible. When you are pleased with photo, save and print to size. **Note:** *On sample project, main photo measures 8 x 11 inches; two smaller photos measure 3¼ x 4⅝ inches.*

Layout: Adhere a 12-inch square of flowers printed paper to a 12-inch-square of orange card stock. Adhere a 2½ x 12-inch strip of circles-and-squares printed paper down left side of layout ¾ inch from left edge. Adhere a 1½ x 12-inch piece of diamonds printed paper horizontally across bottom of layout at a slight angle, 1–1½ inches from bottom edge.

Ink edges of large photo with distress ink; adhere near upper left corner of layout at a slight angle. Print two photos in color to measure 3½ x 4½ inches; ink edges and adhere in lower right corner of layout, overlapping as shown.

Adhere a 12½-inch piece of ribbon across bottom of layout at a slight angle, folding ends over edges and securing on reverse side; staple over ribbons near ends. Adhere card-stock quote sticker over ribbon in lower left corner of layout.

Brush foam uppercase "F" stamp with orange paint; stamp onto transparency; let dry. Brush lowercase "all" with orange, green and gold paints; stamp vertically onto transparency next to "F." As paints dry, they will take on a crackled appearance. Trim transparency around stamped "Fall"; adhere to layout in upper right corner as shown. Adhere "Leaves" card stock sticker to layout below "Fall," overlapping photo. Adhere silk leaf in upper left corner of layout. ■

SOURCES: Printed papers and stickers from Gin-X; transparency from 3M; alphabet stamps from Heidi Swapp; ribbon from Offray; Photoshop Elements 2.0 from Adobe Systems Inc.; adhesive from Beacon.

Materials

3 digital photos or photo print of desired size	Fall-themed card-stock stickers	⅜-inch-wide brown/orange/ green ribbon	Computer font
Photo paper	Printable transparency	Silk fall leaf	Printer
Orange card stock	Brown distress ink	Stapler with silver and orange staples	Paper adhesive
Printed papers in fall colors: flowers, circles-and-squares, diamonds	Acrylic paints: orange, light green, gold	Computer with photo-editing software	
	2½-inch foam alphabet stamps to spell "Fall"		

Leaves

children change
much like the
seasons and it's
best to capture the
innocence of both

SUNDIAL

DESIGN BY SUSAN STRINGFELLOW

Several photos show different viewpoints of the same subject to tell the whole story.

Project note: Adhere elements using permanent adhesive unless instructed otherwise.

Filter photo editing: To give one of the photos the look of a colored-pencil drawing, like the photo of the sundial on the sample layout, open the selected photo within photo-editing program. Go to "Filter," then "Artistic," then select "Colored Pencil." Adjust pencil width and stroke pressure as desired. Save image and print. *Note: On sample project, photo is printed to 6⅞ x 5 inches, including ⅛-inch white borders; complete layout measures 12 inches square.*

Layout: Adhere a 7 x 5½-inch piece of gray squares printed paper to 12-inch square of green printed card stock 1¾ inches from top edge, with right edges even. Adhere a 1 x 12-inch strip of gray circles printed paper down right side of layout, ¼ inch from right edge.

Center a 13-inch length of gray/silver ribbon on a 13-inch length of light green ribbon; adhere across layout ¼ inch from top edge, folding ends over to back and adhering them on reverse side of layout.

Adhere "colored pencil" photo to layout ⅛ inch from left edge and 3½ inches from top edge. Adhere remaining photos to black card stock; cut out, leaving narrow borders. Adhere photos to layout as shown in photo.

Adhere monogram "d" to lower left corner of layout. Adhere "IIX" Roman numeral stickers up left edge of layout as shown; add alphabet circle stickers to spell "sun," adhering them with foam mounting squares.

Using black paint as ink, stamp "ial" onto bottom of layout after monogram "d." Adhere "Time" alphabet stickers to die-cut tag; adhere tag to upper left corner of layout using two decorative fasteners.

Use computer to generate journaling and date onto printable transparency; cut out in separate pieces. Center journaling in upper section of layout; attach using a decorative fastener. Cut 1-inch lengths of both ribbons; fold over and attach with date to lower right corner of layout using a decorative fastener.

Fold over 2-inch lengths of green and gray ribbons; attach over left edge of bottom photo near upper left corner using two decorative fasteners.

SOURCES: Printed card stock from Bazzill; printed papers, tag, monogram and stickers from BasicGrey; transparency from 3M; alphabet stamps from Technique Tuesday; decorative fasteners from EK Success Ltd.; Photoshop from Adobe Systems Inc.

Materials

High-resolution photo on computer disk or digital camera card	2 x 3-inch gray circles printed card-stock tag	Stickers: ¾-inch light gray Roman numerals, ½-inch black alphabet	6 (⅝-inch) silver decorative fasteners
Matte-finish photo paper	4-inch gray squares printed card-stock "d" monogram	1½- to 2-inch alphabet stamps	Computer with photo-editing software
Card stock: green print, solid black	Printable transparency	Black acrylic paint	Color printer
Printed paper: gray squares, gray circles	1-inch alphabet circles to spell "sun"	Ribbons: ⅝-inch-wide light green, 5/16-inch-wide silver/gray	Adhesive foam mounting squares
			Permanent adhesive

Time

ix sun

dial

This is the Sundial at the Museum of Natural Science. I was taking photos of Chris and I noticed that the minute the sun came out from behind a cloud and the sundial formed a shadow, Chris looked at his watch to see if it was right!

This sundial is a large gnomon with a lens which focuses the noonday sun near the equinoxes. Hour lines were designed to compensate for the equation of time.

Materials

Digital photo

Glossy-finish photo paper

Card stock: black, deep red

Cream/sage/burgundy/gold/
  brown printed paper: stripes,
  polka dots

Distress ink

Rub-on transfers:
  "live laugh love"

Die-cut "live well, laugh often,
  love much" tag

Computer with photo-editing
  software

Printer

Paper adhesive

LIVE, LAUGH, LOVE

DESIGN BY TAMI MAYBERRY

Using digital imaging software, alter photos to coordinate with special papers.

Photo: Open photo within photo-editing program. Select "Enhance" option in main (top) toolbar; choose "Adjust Color" and click on "Hue/Saturation." Slide "Saturation" bar to the left, reducing color to desired intensity; click "OK."

Select "Layer and Duplicate Layer" option from main toolbar. Click "OK" in pop-up window to duplicate layer. Select "Image" function from main toolbar; choose "Adjust Color" option and click to remove color.

Select Eraser tool from tool palette; erase desired portion of top layer to reveal colored bottom layer. Save photo and print, sizing photo to 4½ x 6¾ inches.

Layout: Center and adhere an 8¼ x 10¾-inch piece of striped printed paper (cut with stripes running vertically) to an 8½ x 11-inch piece of black card stock.

Center and adhere an 8¼ x 2¼-inch strip of polka-dot printed paper to an 8¼ x 2½-inch strip of black card stock. Ink edges of strip with distress ink. Apply "live," "laugh" and "love" rub-on transfers to half-circles in strip as shown in photo. Adhere strip across layout ⅝ inch from bottom edge.

Center and adhere photo to deep red card stock and trim, leaving ⅛-inch borders. Adhere matted photo to black card stock and trim, leaving ⅛-inch borders. Adhere matted photo to layout 1¹¹⁄₁₆ inch from left edge and ⁵⁄₁₆ inch from top edge.

Adhere die-cut tag to layout to right of photo, 2½ inches from top edge and ½ inch from right edge. ∎

SOURCES: Printed papers and die-cut tag from Three Bugs in a Rug; rub-on transfers from Royal & Langnickel; Photoshop Elements from Adobe Systems Inc.

The original photograph contained a distracting background and colors too bright for the printed paper the designer chose to use.

Materials

Digital photo

Glossy-finish photo paper

Digital printed paper: gray, blue swirls

Digital blue mini brad image

Digital swirl image

Computer with photo-editing software

Printer

WINTER BEAUTY

DESIGN BY TAMI MAYBERRY

A stark black-and-white photo in a simple digital layout offers breathtaking beauty.

Layout: Open green printed paper image within photo-editing software. Click on "Enhance" option in main toolbar; select "Adjust Color" and click on "Remove Color."

Click on "Enhance" option in main toolbar; select "Adjust Color" and click on "Color Variations." With "Intensity" set at midlevel, choose "Midtones" option. Click on "Increase Blue"; click on "Decrease Red." Click "Lighten" option twice; click "OK."

Open blue swirl printed paper image within graphics program. Click on "Enhance" option in main toolbar; select "Adjust Color" and click on "Color Variations." With "Intensity" set at midlevel, choose "Midtones" option. Click five times on "Darken" feature. Select "Highlights" option; click "Darken" feature twice.

Select "Shadows" option; click "Lighten" feature twice. Select "Highlights" option; click on "Decrease Green"; click "OK."

Select Rectangular Marquee tool from tool palette. Just below main toolbar, click on "Mode" drop-down box; set to "Fixed" size. Adjust width to 12 inches wide x 3 inches high. Click on image.

Select Move tool from tool palette. Drag and drop highlighted area of swirl pattern onto main layout. Maximize layout window; center border on page as desired.

Open desired photo. Click on "Enhance" option in main toolbar; select "Adjust Color" and click on "Remove Color." Select Move tool from tool palette; drag and drop photo image onto main layout.

With photo area still highlighted, click "Layer" on main toolbar; click "Arrange" option. Click on "Bring to Front" to bring photo to front of page. Position photo as desired.

Select Eyedropper tool from tool palette; click on photo to select.

Click on curved arrow beside color palette, changing foreground color to white. Click on "Edit" function in main toolbar; click "Stroke" option. Adjust settings to read as follows: Width: 30 px; Location: inside; Blending Mode: normal; Opacity: 100 percent. Click "OK."

Click on curved arrow beside color palette, changing foreground color to blue. Click on "Edit" function in main toolbar; click "Stroke" option. Adjust settings to read as follows: Width: 20 px; Location: center; Blending Mode: normal; Opacity: 100 percent. Click "OK."

Click on swirl border to select. Click on "Edit" function in main toolbar; click "Stroke" option. Adjust settings to read as follows: Width: 20 px; Location: center; Blending Mode: normal; Opacity: 100 percent. Click "OK."

Select Rectangular Marquee tool from tool palette. Just below main toolbar, click on "Mode" drop-down box; set to "Normal." Click on top left corner of image. Hold down left mouse button and drag to highlight outer edge of image. Right-click on image; click on "Stroke" option. Adjust settings to read as follows: Width: 20 px; Location: center; Blending Mode: normal; Opacity: 100 percent. Click "OK."

CONTINUED ON PAGE 168

A Small Sign of SPRING

SIGN OF SPRING

DESIGN BY TAMI MAYBERRY

Bright yellow dandelions, combined with matching
paper and embellishments, spring off the page.

Project note: Adhere photos and paper using paper adhesive. Adhere chipboard embellishments using craft glue.

Photos: Open photo image within photo-editing software. Click on "Layer and Duplicate Layer" option in main toolbar; click "OK" in pop-up window to duplicate layer.

Select "Image" function in main toolbar; choose "Adjust Color" and click on "Remove Color." Increase brightness level and decrease contrast level. Click "OK."

Select Eraser in tool palette. Erase desired portion of top layer to reveal colored bottom layer. Save and print photos. *Note: On sample layout, main photo measures 7 x 5 inches; accent photo measures 3 x 4 inches; complete layout measures 12 inches square.*

Layout: Spray chipboard flower with yellow paint; spray arrow with teal. When dry, scratch petal details onto flower using straight pin.

Center and adhere an 11¾ x 10-inch piece of teal card stock to 12-inch square of white card stock ¾ inch from top edge. Center and adhere an 11 x 8-inch piece of yellow card stock over teal card stock 2 inches from top of layout.

Center and adhere a 10¾ x 8½-inch piece of printed paper to page 1 inch from top edge. Center and adhere a 10 x ¼-inch strip of teal card stock to layout ½ inch from bottom of page. Attach flower brads to layout at ends of strip.

Adhere main photo to teal card stock; trim, leaving ³⁄₁₆-inch borders. Adhere photo to layout 2¼ inches from left edge and 1⅜ inches from top edge. Adhere smaller photo to layout as shown, overlapping edge of main photo. Apply rub-on transfers to spell "A Small Sign of SPRING" to yellow card stock below photos.

Adhere chipboard arrow over smaller photo as shown. Adhere turquoise brad to center of chipboard flower; adhere flower to upper left corner of layout. ■

SOURCES: Printed paper from Autumn Leaves; rub-on transfers from Royal & Langnickel; paint from Krylon; chipboard embellishments from Majestic Memories; brads from Creative Impressions and Queen & Co.; Photoshop Elements from Adobe Systems Inc.

Materials

2 complementary digital photos	Dark blue rub-on transfers: alphabet, "SPRING"	Decorative brads: ½-inch turquoise "2" brad, 2 (⅝-inch) yellow flowers	Computer with photo-editing software
Glossy-finish photo paper	Spray paint: teal, yellow	Straight pin	Printer
Card stock: white, teal, yellow	Chipboard embellishments: 2½-inch flower, 5-inch arrow		Paper adhesive
Blue floral printed paper			Craft glue

Materials

Photos: 5 x 7-inch, 3 or 4 photos 3–4 inches x 1⅞ inch

Card stock to complement printed papers

Printed papers: green/white polka dots, pink floral, pink/green/white stripes, solid pink

Printable transparency

1- to 3-inch foam flower stamps

Pastel craft paints: blue, green, pink

1-inch round "B" sticker

Silver metal floral embellishments: 1½-inch round frame, 1 x 1-inch corner bracket

Dragonfly paper clip

1½ x ¾-inch pink metal bookplate

2 lavender flower brads

Sewing machine with white thread

Foam brushes

Label maker

Sandpaper

Paper adhesive

Craft cement

Computer with fonts of your choice

Printer

BEST BUDS

DESIGN BY SHERRY WRIGHT

Four small photos help frame a larger one in this study of sisters.

Project note: Adhere all elements using paper adhesive unless instructed otherwise.

Adhere a 12-inch square of striped paper to a 12-inch square of card stock. Brush foam flower stamps with pink, blue and green paints using foam brush; stamp flower images randomly over layout, stamping several flowers without reapplying paint for a shadow-stamped effect. Dry-brush edges of layout with green paint.

Dry-brush edges of a 12 x 4-inch rectangle of polka-dot paper and a 12 x 2½-inch strip of floral paper. Randomly stamp floral paper with pink, blue and green flowers. Center and adhere floral paper to polka-dot paper. Machine-stitch two crisscrossing wavy lines over top seam between papers using a straight stitch; over bottom seam, machine-stitch using a feather stitch. Adhere entire piece to layout near bottom edge.

Dry-brush edges of a 7 x 3½-inch piece of polka-dot paper with blue paint; randomly stamp paper with blue and pink flowers. Adhere paper to upper right quadrant of layout 1 inch from top edge and right edges even.

Adhere photo to left side of layout ½ inch from top edge and ⅞ inch from left edge. Adhere remaining photos across layered strip at bottom of layout, overlapping photos as needed to make a continuous photo strip.

Use computer to generate "bud" using 3- to 4¼-inch font of your choice; print out on plain paper and cut out.

Using paper templates, cut letters from assorted printed papers. Dry-brush edges and stamp with flowers using pink, blue and green paints as desired. Adhere letters to 7 x 3½-inch polka-dot paper in upper right quadrant, overlapping and intertwining letters as desired.

Use computer to generate journaling to fit within open space below "bud" panel (on sample, 6⅛ x 2½ inches). Print onto transparency; trim and adhere to layout.

Stamp large blue flower onto floral paper; cut out. Adhere to upper left corner of layout, over corner of photo. Adhere "B" sticker to center of flower. Brush metal round frame, corner bracket and dragonfly paper clip with green paint; sand edges. Adhere metal frame around "B" sticker on flower using craft cement. Adhere corner bracket over lower right corner of photo using craft cement. Slide paper clip over top edge of bottom polka-dot paper strip, 2½ inches to right of large photo.

Run a ¼-inch-wide strip of solid pink card stock through label maker and imprint with year; dry-brush edges and year with green paint. Adhere strip to lower right corner of layout below photo strip, ¼ inch from right edge. Frame strip with pink bookplate; affix bookplate to layout with flower brads. ■

SOURCES: Printed papers, sticker and bookplate from Making Memories; foam stamps from Heidi Swapp; metal embellishments and paper clip from Nunn Design; flower brads from Queen & Co.; paper adhesive from Beacon.

laughing

joy

quirky

wacky

awesome   zany

rowdy

wild   noisy

GO ahead &

JUMP!

12/04

JUMP

DESIGN BY STEPHANIE BARNARD

Word tiles and shiny metal embellishments draw attention
to high-contrast black-and-white photos.

Project notes: Adhere card stock, paper, photos and stickers with double-sided tape. Adhere other elements with adhesive dots.,

Adhere a 12 x 5¾-inch piece of striped card stock across bottom half of a 12-inch-square sheet of printed paper. Center a 7½ x 14-inch piece of metal screen over left half of layout; bend excess screen over to reverse side along left edge, top and bottom edges.

Adhere photos to an 8⅝-inch square of solid black card stock as shown; adhere word stickers in margins. Adhere photo panel to upper left corner of layout. Die-cut letters and exclamation point to spell "JUMP!" from light portions of additional printed paper; adhere to lower right corner of layout. Affix alphabet bottle caps to spell "GO," metal letters to spell "ahead," and metal ampersand over screen in lower left corner of layout as shown using adhesive dots. Add date in gray area of striped card stock with rubber stamps and ink. ■

SOURCES: Card stock from DMD Industries; printed paper, card-stock stickers and bottle caps from Design Originals; rubber stamps from JustRite Stampers/Millennium Marking Co.; screen from AMACO; metal discs from Making Memories and Colorbök; die-cutting machine and dies from Ellison/Sizzix; adhesive dots and tape from Beacon.

Materials

Glossy-finish black-and-white photos: 4⅝ x 7-inch, 3⅜ x 5-inch, 2 x 3-inch	Black-and-white diamonds printed paper	Black ink pad	¾-inch silver metal disc with ampersand
Card stock: black, gray/black striped	Card-stock word stickers: gray, white, black	1¼-inch alphabet bottle caps to spell "GO"	Die-cutting tool with 1½- to 2-inch alphabet dies
	Diamond-mesh metal screen	½-inch silver metal alphabet discs to spell "ahead"	Adhesive dots
	¼-inch numeral rubber stamps		Double-sided tape

Watching Ashley

GROW

It is so hard to believe that you are nine years old already. You have grown so fast. It seems like just yesterday that we were in the car playing games to teach you new words. Now, we spend those trips in the car listening to you talk about boys. Oh my! I know I can't stop you from growing up but but it sure would be nice if I could slow it down a bit. You are such a precious gift to me and I hope to spend many more years sharing your life and watching you grow.

JULY 2004

Materials

5 x 7-inch photo

Card stock: purple, teal, light green, dark lavender

Green/teal/purple plaid printed paper

Distress ink

Fine-tip black marker (optional)

White rub-on alphabet transfers: 1-inch capital letters, ³/₈-inch upper- and lowercase letters

3 lavender flower buttons

2 purple flower shank buttons or charms

3 teal flower brads

Teal bookplate

2 purple mini brads

³/₁₆- to ¼-inch-wide ribbons: purple-and-white gingham check, lavender with white pin dots

Chartreuse rickrack

Craft nippers

Stapler with staples

Paper adhesive

Craft cement

Computer with font of your choice

Printer

WATCHING ASHLEY GROW

DESIGN BY TAMI MAYBERRY

Snippets of ribbon and a bit of journaling turn an ordinary moment into a precious memory.

Project note: *Adhere elements using paper adhesive unless instructed otherwise.*

Ink edges of an 8 x 10⅛-inch piece of plaid printed paper with distress ink; adhere to 12-inch square of dark lavender card stock ⅜ inch from top and left edges. Adhere a 4½ x 5½-inch piece of teal card stock to layout ⅜ inch from top edge and ¼ inch from right edge. Ink edges of an 8 x 5¾-inch piece of light green card stock with distress ink; adhere to layout ¼ inch from right edge and 5⁄16 inch from bottom edge. Adhere a 3¼ x 1½-inch piece of teal card stock to layout 5⁄16 inch from bottom edge and ⅜ inch from left edge.

Adhere a 4½ x 6½-inch piece of teal card stock to layout over plaid printed paper, ¾ inch from top and left edges of layout. Adhere three 1-inch squares of teal card stock to purple card stock; cut out, leaving ⅛-inch purple borders. Adhere squares, evenly spaced, to teal card stock, 1¼ inches from left edge of layout. Adhere a flower button to each square using craft cement; snap shanks off flower charms and adhere one to center flower button using craft cement.

Ribbon fringe: Cut a 6⅝ x 7½-inch rectangle from purple card stock. Cut 15 (3-inch) pieces from each ribbon; arrange ribbons in 10 groups of three down left edge of teal card stock, alternating ribbon colors and allowing one end of each piece to extend beyond left edge of teal card stock by about 1½ inches. Staple down left edge of card stock across centers of ribbon groups, positioning staples parallel to left edge of card stock, about ¼ inch from edge. Tie each ribbon around staple; trim ribbon ends.

Adhere ribbon-fringed panel to layout 2½ inches from right edge and 1⅛ inches from top edge. Adhere photo to teal card stock; trim, leaving ⅛-inch borders. Adhere photo to ribbon-fringed card-stock panel ⅛ inch from top, right and bottom edges.

Adhere a 7½ x 1½-inch strip of plaid printed paper to right side of layout, against edge of purple card stock. Apply rub-on transfer letters to spell "GROW" to four 1¼ x 1½-inch rectangles of purple card stock. Adhere "G" rectangle to plaid strip ⅛ inch from top, right and left edges of strip. Adhere remaining letters to strip, spacing them ⅛ inch apart.

Apply rub-on transfers to spell "Watching Ashley" to top right corner of layout, just over photo and "GROW" panels. Adhere remaining charm to layout to right of transfers. Attach teal flower brads, evenly spaced, to light green card stock, in a vertical row to right of "W" in "GROW."

Use computer to generate, or hand-print, journaling onto teal card stock to fit within an area measuring approximately 5½ x 2¼ inches. Print out and trim around words, centering them in a 7 x 2½-inch rectangle. Adhere rectangle over light green card stock in lower right corner of layout, ½ inch from right edge and ¾ inch from bottom edge.

Apply rub-on transfers for date to teal card stock in lower left corner of layout. Attach teal bookplate to card stock using purple mini brads, framing date. Adhere chartreuse rickrack down left side of layout ½ inch from edge using craft cement. ■

SOURCES: Printed paper, buttons and small rub-on transfers from Doodlebug Design Inc.; large rub-on transfers, flower brads, bookplate and mini brads from Making Memories.

SWEET LOVE

DESIGN BY KRISTEN SWAIN

Trimmed printed paper becomes a graphic element to frame two matted photos in this elegant layout.

Project note: Adhere elements using paper adhesive unless instructed otherwise.

Center and adhere a 10¾-inch square of polka-dot paper to a 12-inch square of pink card stock. Center and adhere 12 x ⅜-inch strips of red card stock to pink card-stock border as shown, crisscrossing strips in corners.

Adhere photos to salmon card stock and trim, leaving ⅛-inch borders. Adhere photos to layout as shown, overlapping slightly. Trim around two floral motifs from floral printed paper; adhere motifs in upper right and lower left corners as shown, trimming outer edges even with edges of layout, and slightly overlapping corner of top photo.

Use computer and printer to generate journaling onto transparency to fit within an area approximately 4 x 1½ inches. Trim around journaling and adhere to layout in lower right corner, below bottom photo. Cut two 2 x 2-inch photo corners from salmon card stock; adhere over lower right and upper left corners of polka-dot paper panel. Knot two pieces of ribbon; trim ends at an angle and adhere to photo corners using craft glue.

Cut two 2 x ½-inch strips from red card stock; fold in half and sandwich left edge of top photo between ends; attach strips to photo and layout with mini brads.

Using a sans serif font, print outlines of 2¼-inch-tall letters to spell "SWEET" onto salmon card stock. Using a script-style font, print outline of ½- to ¾-inch-tall words "of mine" onto red card stock. Using a craft knife, cut out letters and words. Adhere alphabet stickers to spell "love" on red card stock; using craft knife, cut out individual letters, leaving very narrow borders. Adhere "SWEET" to layout just below top photo; adhere matted "love" stickers, overlapping "SWEET" as shown. Adhere "of mine" below "love," slightly overlapping left edge of lower photo.

Stamp ghost heart with handwriting background image; let dry. Adhere heart to red card stock and cut out; adhere to layout, overlapping top edge of lower photo near upper right corner. ■

SOURCES: Printed paper and alphabet stickers from Bo-Bunny Press; transparency from 3M; stamp from PSX; pigment ink from Tsukineko; ghost heart from Heidi Swapp; ribbon from Li'l Davis Designs.

Materials

2 color photos: 5½ x 4-inch, 4 x 4¾-inch	Handwriting background stamp	2 black mini brads	Computer with serif, sans serif, and script fonts of your choice
Card stock: pink, red, salmon	Black pigment ink	³/₁₆-inch-wide rose-with-white-polka-dots grosgrain ribbon	Printer
Cream/red printed papers: polka dots, floral	1¼-inch black-and-red polka-dot alphabet stickers to spell "love"	Craft knife and mat	
Printable transparency	1½ x 2-inch ghost heart	Paper adhesive	
		Craft glue	

SWEET love of mine

Annalise is such a wonderful baby, she's so happy and alert, hardly crying, just wanting to be in the midst of whatever is happening. Just barely 5 months old, she's enjoying her first foods and starting to crawl. I enjoy each new discovery with her, wanting to see life through her innocent eyes, wanting to remember each and every moment of this wonderful but short time of her life.

summer '74

JEREMY SuSie JEREMY SuSie JEREMY SuSie JEREMY SuSie JEREMY SuSie JEREMY SuSie JEREMY SuSie

{OH BROTHER}

so happy

love

no more pictures today

OH, BROTHER

DESIGN BY SUSAN STRINGFELLOW

Pouting and temper tantrums are guaranteed during childhood, so why not document a few for the next generation?

Project note: Adhere elements using paper adhesive unless instructed otherwise.

Use computer to print children's names in a 6-inch circle near right edge of an 8½ x 11-inch piece of white card stock, 1¼ inches from top edge. Adhere a 5-inch circle of floral printed paper to card stock inside name circle. Trim top edge of a 1 x 11-inch strip of striped paper using decorative-edge scissors; adhere strip to layout ¼ inch from left edge.

Tag: Stamp "OH BROTHER" onto card-stock tag; stamp "not" in front of "so happy" at bottom of tag. Die-cut brackets from black card stock; adhere to tag around "OH BROTHER." Knot a 4-inch piece of ribbon through hole in tag; adhere tag to lower left corner of layout, leaving ribbon ends free for now.

Lightly pencil position of photo onto layout. Die-cut flourishes from green/white printed paper; adhere above photo position and at lower left corner so that photo will overlap flourishes somewhat. Punch a few tiny flowers from red card stock; adhere to flourishes. Adhere photo to layout.

Adhere coordinating tab over top edge of layout near upper right corner; it will protrude from top. Write date on tab using fine-tip marker. Center a 5-inch piece of star trim over left edge of photo, overlapping photo slightly, and adhere to layout using craft glue. Adhere 1¼-inch circle sticker over right edge of photo near upper corner.

Machine-stitch around edges of layout using black thread and a mixture of straight and zigzag stitches; machine-stitch along right edge of tag using straight stitch. Wrap ribbon ends over left edge and secure on reverse side. Secure ribbon ends on front of layout using decorative brad. Add journaling to 1½-inch red circle tag with black fine-tip marker; attach tag to ribbon using safety pin. ∎

SOURCES: Printed papers, tab and tags from SEI; stamps from Purple Onion Designs; brad from Chatterbox; star trim from Making Memories; ribbon from American Crafts; punch from Carl; die-cutting machine and dies from QuicKutz Inc.

Materials

6 x 4-inch color photo	1¼-inch round floral sticker	⅜-inch wide orange-with-white-pin-dots ribbon	Paper adhesive
Card stock: white, black, red	1½-inch red round tag		Craft glue
Printed papers: orange/red/green floral, green/white print, green/orange/red stripe	¼-inch alphabet stamps	⁵⁄₁₆-inch flower punch	Computer with font of your choice
	Black ink pad	Die-cutting machine	Printer
	Black fine-tip marker	Dies: 1½-inch brackets, flourish	
Coordinating card-stock embellishments: green with white polka-dots tag, striped tab	Green decorative brad	Decorative-edge scissors	
	1-inch black safety pin	Sewing machine with black thread	
	⅝-inch-wide white star trim		

EMBRACE IT

DESIGN BY RACHAEL GIALLONGO

A close-up action photo is the centerpiece of a simple digital layout.

Download and unzip digital scrapbook kit. Open photo-editing program. Click "File," then "New" to create 12-inch-square canvas at 300 dpi.

Open photo file. Crop as desired, and then size image to 6 x 9½ inches at 300 dpi.

Open folders containing the digital scrapbooking components. Use Drag tool to layer printed papers, text and other elements as shown. Use Brush tool to "tea-stain" elements and title. Add journaling text. Add drop shadows along bottom and right-hand edges of paper "layers" for the most realistic appearance.

Save file with JPEG extension at a quality of 10 for best printing results. Print layout onto glossy-finish photo paper. ■

SOURCES: Robin Carlton & Christy Lyle digital scrapbook kit from www. SweetShoppeDesigns.com; Christine Smith digital tea-staining kit from www. TheDigiChick.com; Photoshop 7.0 from Adobe Systems Inc.

Materials

Digital photo	Digital scrapbooking kit	Computer with photo-editing	Fonts of your choice
Wide-format glossy-finish photo paper	Digital "tea-staining" kit	software	Wide-format printer

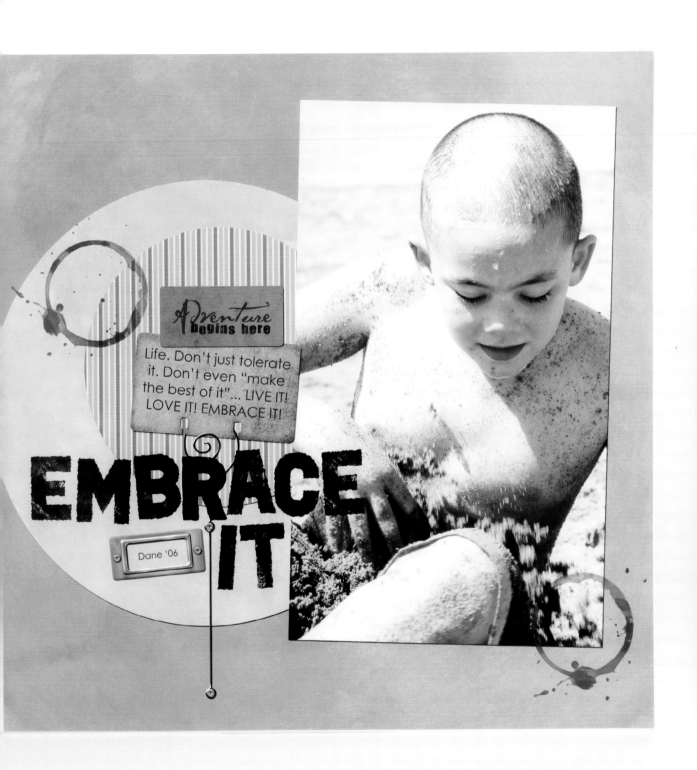

Adventure begins here

Life. Don't just tolerate it. Don't even "make the best of it"... LIVE IT! LOVE IT! EMBRACE IT!

EMBRACE IT

Dane '06

always – forever

we
r
fAMIly

WE R FAMILY

DESIGN BY SHERRY WRIGHT

Shake things up with unusual photo placement, a fun font treatment and lots of coordinating embellishments.

Project note: Adhere photo and paper using paper adhesive. Adhere remaining elements using craft glue.

Open digital photo on computer; convert image to black-and-white. Crop image and size to 8½ x 12 inches; print. **Note:** *On sample project, photo is printed in landscape mode.* Adhere photo to 12-inch square of black card stock ⅛ inch from right edge and ⅝ inch from bottom edge.

Trim around images in 12-inch square of floral printed paper to create "frame" for photo along left side and across top and bottom, overlapping edges of photo as desired; adhere to layout.

Adhere transparent flower sticker to photo where paper floral motifs end, on right edge of page. Embellish cut edges of paper with rickrack as desired. Adhere chipboard letters to spell "we r family" to paper along left side of layout, mixing uppercase and lowercase letters as desired and altering orientation of a letter or two.

Punch hearts from solid light blue and light green printed papers. Overlap light blue heart onto light green heart; adhere hearts to lower right corner of layout. Push "true" brad through center of paper flower; adhere to light blue heart. Using black glaze pen, outline overlapped hearts, "we" chipboard letters and individual motifs within printed paper as desired; add journaling to printed paper along curved edges, next to rickrack. ■

SOURCES: Printed paper from Cherry Arte; chipboard alphabet and flower sticker from Heidi Swapp; brad from Queen & Co.; glaze pen from Sakura.

Materials

Digital photo	1⅜- to 2-inch black chipboard	Black glaze pen or fine-tip pen	Computer with photo-editing
Glossy photo paper	alphabet	½-inch turquoise "true" brad	software
Black card stock	Light green paper flower	Lime green rickrack	Printer
Printed papers: blue/green/white	Transparent sticker with white	Paper adhesive	
floral, light green, solid light blue	"hand-drawn" flower	Craft glue	

Materials

6 x 4-inch color photo

White card stock

Printed papers: brown/white/
green circles, blue

Card-stock stickers: green "HERE
COMES TROUBLE," brown oval
"Attitude," border with words

Green print 5 x 1½-inch card-
stock tag

2½-inch white chipboard "A"

Corrugated cardboard

1¼-inch "e" stamp

Ink pads: blue, black

Blue watercolor paint

Black fine-tip marker

4 "antique" mini brads

2 (½-inch) silver washer-style
eyelets

2 (7/16-inch-wide) printed
grosgrain ribbons

Fine macramé twine

Watercolor brush

Corner rounder punch

Eyelet-setting tool

Paper adhesive

Adhesive foam tape

Computer with font of
your choice

Printer

ALEX

DESIGN BY SUSAN STRINGFELLOW

Capture the essence of your child's personality with one perfect photo and a favorite verse.

Project note: Adhere elements using paper adhesive unless instructed otherwise.

Use computer to generate, or hand-print, favorite quotation, poem, etc., in lower right corner of an 8½ x 11-inch piece of white card stock within an area measuring approximately 3¼ x 2¾ inches. Brush blue watercolor paint around edges of card stock; lightly brush watercolor highlight over a key word. Ink edges of card stock with blue ink.

Round off corners on a 5 x 10½-inch piece of brown printed paper; center and adhere to left side of layout ¼ inch from left edge. Round off upper left and lower right corners on a 7½ x 5¼-inch rectangle of blue printed paper and on photo; adhere paper to layout 1 inch from top edge and ¾ inch from left edge. Adhere photo to white card stock and trim, leaving ³⁄₁₆-inch borders. Adhere photo to blue paper panel ¼ inch from right edge and ⁵⁄₁₆ inch from top edge. Cut three words from border sticker; adhere over left edge of photo and add a mini brad to one end of each strip.

Adhere "HERE COMES TROUBLE" sticker vertically to lower left corner of layout, 1 inch from bottom edge and ⅛ inch from left edge. Using adhesive foam tape, adhere "Attitude" sticker to layout ¾ inch from bottom edge and overlapping "trouble" sticker as shown.

Name tag: Attach eyelet to each end of green tag; knot ribbons through eyelets. Spell name on tag using a variety of materials for letters. Sample shows a white chipboard "A," inked along edges and brushed with watercolor along one edge; name has been added using fine-tip marker. "L" is formed from a double 3-inch strand of fine macramé twine, knotted together at ends and affixed to tag with mini brad. "E" is stamped onto tag using black ink. "X" is formed by adhering sanded, crisscrossing strips of corrugated cardboard to tag. Adhere tag to layout below photo and ¾ inch from right edge. ■

SOURCES: Printed papers, card-stock stickers and tag from Fancy Pants Designs; chipboard "A" from Pressed Petals; stamp from Sugarloaf Products; eyelets from We R Memory Keepers; ribbons from American Crafts; twine from The Beadery; adhesive foam tape from 3M.

KOALA

DESIGN BY SHERRY WRIGHT

Personalize your page title to reflect whatever costume your little one is wearing.

Project note: *Adhere elements using paper adhesive unless instructed otherwise.*

Adhere a 12-inch square of circles paper to a 12-inch square of card stock. Ink edges of a 10 x 7-inch piece of leaves paper; adhere to layout near top of page ½ inch from left edge. Adhere a 12 x 2-inch strip of blocks paper down right side of layout ¾ inch from right edge. Adhere a 7 x 2-inch rectangle of leaves paper to lower right corner of layout, overlapping blocks strip.

Center and adhere photo to layout 2½ inches from left edge, leaving an opening along center of right edge for inserting tag.

Ink edges of chipboard alphabet tiles; adhere down left side of layout ³⁄₁₆ inch from photo using craft glue. Cut leaf motifs from printed paper using craft knife; adhere over upper right and lower left corners of photo.

Tag: Cut leaves paper to cover top 2 inches of tag; adhere. Cut a darker green leaves motif from paper; adhere to tag so that it extends beyond top edge. Add journaling to tag using fine-tip marker. Slide tag behind photo through opening along right edge, leaving top of tag protruding. ■

SOURCES: Printed papers from Mara-Mi Inc. and Paper Salon; chipboard tiles from Making Memories; adhesive from Beacon.

Materials

8¼ x 10¾-inch color photo	block outlines, green/white/	1½-inch-square chipboard	Paper adhesive
Brown card stock	blue leaves	alphabet tiles to spell "koala":	Craft glue
Printed papers: brown/white	3-inch-wide manila shipping tag	green, blue	
small circles, brown/white	Brown ink	Craft knife	

DRAMA

DESIGN BY TAMI MAYBERRY

Document your drama queen's most flamboyant performance with large chipboard letters and pastel papers.

Center and adhere a 10¾ x 8-inch rectangle of striped paper to an 11 x 8½-inch sheet of white card stock. Adhere a 3 x 7½-inch rectangle of orange swirl paper to layout 2¾ inches from left edge with top edge even with top edge of striped paper.

Sand edges of chipboard letters. Apply rub-on transfers to spell "PURE" onto chipboard "D"; adhere chipboard letters to layout with bottom edges even with left edge of orange swirl paper.

Adhere an 8 x 6½-inch rectangle of floral printed paper to layout ¾ inch from top edge, aligning right edges of floral and striped papers. Adhere a 1¼ x 7¼-inch strip of striped paper to layout 3¼ inches from left edge and with top and bottom edges even with top and bottom edges of underlying orange swirl paper.

Adhere photo to card stock; trim, leaving narrow borders. Ink edges of card stock; adhere photo to layout 1¼ inches from top edge with right edge even with right edge of underlying printed papers.

Adhere an 8-inch piece of rickrack across layout just below photo. Attach flower brads to lower right corner of layout, ½ inch from right and bottom edges. ■

SOURCES: Printed paper from BasicGrey; chipboard letters from Pressed Petals; rub-on transfers from Doodlebug Design Inc.; flower brads and rickrack from Creative Impressions.

Materials

7 x 5-inch color photo	orange swirl	¼-inch bright pink alphabet	Fine sandpaper
White card stock	2½-inch pink chipboard letters	rub-on transfers	Paper adhesive
Orange/pink/green printed	to spell "DRAMA"	3 (⅝-inch) white flower brads	
papers: diagonal stripe, floral,	Orange ink pad	Bright orange rickrack	

UNMANAGEABLE BOY

DESIGN BY RACHAEL GIALLONGO

Symmetrical shapes framed by a black background draw the eye to a special photograph.

Project note: Adhere photo, paper and card stock using paper adhesive. Adhere chipboard pieces and remaining elements using craft glue.

Round off corners of photo and a 4¼ x 8½-inch rectangle of gold card stock. Center and adhere photo to card stock ⅛ inch from top edge. Round off corners on a 12-inch square of black card stock; center and adhere photo panel to card stock 1⅝ inches from top edge.

Cut three 2-inch squares from light green card stock and four from printed paper; round off all corners. Arrange card stock squares, paper squares and coaster around photo as shown; adhere.

Trim notches in ends of an 11-inch piece of black-and-white pin-dot ribbon; adhere across bottom row of elements as shown. Thread charm onto a 3-inch piece of reversible ribbon; knot and trim ends at an angle. Adhere charm to upper right corner of lower green square on right side.

Apply "giggle" rub-on transfer to chipboard heart frame as shown in photo. Sand edges of heart frame; back with green card stock and adhere over bottom right corner of photo panel. Set mini brad in center of gold paper flower; adhere to lower right corner of heart frame.

Set mini brads in center of remaining flowers; adhere blue flower to black chipboard square. Adhere square to lower left corner of upper right green square.

Apply numeral rub-on transfer to a small piece of gold card stock; trim to fit behind black chipboard frame. Adhere over left edge of bottom striped square on left side. Adhere green flower over left edge of frame and fabric-covered button over right edge.

Add name, dates, journaling, etc., using fine-tip marker. ∎

SOURCES: Printed paper from Scenic Route Paper Co.; chipboard heart frame from Top Line Creations; chipboard square frame and square from Heidi Swapp; chipboard coaster from Imagination Project/Gin-X; paper flowers from Prima; rub-on transfers from American Crafts and Autumn Leaves; soft charm from Around the Block Products; ribbons from Offray.

Of all of the **animals**, the boy is the most **unmanageable.**
—Plato

Dane

giggle

Materials

4 x 6-inch color photo

Card stock: black, sage, gold

Blue/green/gold/red/white striped printed paper

Chipboard embellishments: 2 x 2½-inch barn-red heart frame, 1-inch-square black frame,

1-inch black square, 1⅞-inch-square boy-themed coaster

⅞-inch paper flowers: light green, gold, turquoise

Rub-on transfers: "giggle," ⁹⁄₁₆-inch dark red numeral

1¼-inch round soft "Happy" charm

3 white mini brads

⁹⁄₁₆-inch black-and-white fabric-covered button

Ribbons: 1-inch-wide white-and-black pin-dot grosgrain,

⅜-inch-wide reversible green/gold

Corner rounder punch

Fine sandpaper

Paper adhesive

Craft glue

HAPPY

DESIGN BY TAMI MAYBERRY

One black-and-white photo, one word, lots of dots— it all adds up to a fun and fanciful layout.

Adhere a 7 x 10¾-inch piece of polka-dot card stock to an 8½ x 11-inch piece of striped card stock 1 inch from left edge with top edges even. Machine-stitch down both side edges of polka-dot card stock using white thread and zigzag stitch.

Adhere a 4½ x 8½-inch piece of blue card stock to layout 1¾ inches from left edge with top edges even. Adhere a 3½ x 8½-inch piece of light green card stock to layout ½ inch from top and left edges of blue card-stock panel. Attach photo turn to polka-dot card stock with green mini brad 1 inch below upper left corner of blue card stock so that it overlaps edges of both blue and light green card-stock panels.

Adhere photo to upper right corner of layout. Trim "Happy" die cut to 3 x 1½ inches; adhere to blue card stock and trim, leaving ⅛-inch borders. Adhere to light green card-stock panel below photo. Adhere an 8½ x ¼-inch strip of blue card stock to layout 1 inch from bottom edge, attaching green mini brad at each end. ■

SOURCES: Printed card stock and die cut from My Mind's Eye; mini brads and photo turn from Creative Impressions.

Materials

7 x 6-inch black-and-white
    photo
Printed card stock: green stripe,
    linen/blue/light green polka
    dots

Solid-color card stock: blue,
    light green
"Happy" die cut
3 green mini brads
Green photo turn

Sewing machine with white
    thread
Paper adhesive

Toddler's Rules

mine **b**

mine

If I like it, it's **mine.**

If it's in my hand, it's **mine.**

mine

If I had it a little while ago, it's **mine.**

If it's **mine** it must NEVER appear to be **mine** in any way.

If it looks just like **mine**, it is **mine.**

If I saw it first, it's **mine.**

mine

If you are playing with something and you put it down, it automatically becomes **mine.**

If it's broken, it's yours.

2

Before you were born I read all the parenting books, took classes, and was as ready as I could be for a first time mom. I knew I wouldn't get as much sleep and life would never be the same. But all the books in the world don't prepare you for motherhood. I had no idea what true exhaustion was or how much I could love until you came along. All my well thought out plans went out the window. You would never watch tv, only eat organic foods, and only educational toys would be allowed in our house. Well we've made it through the baby years and here we are in full blown toddlerhood. Sometime in the last six months my sweet baby boy has been replaced by an alter ego that appears without warning. It's usually triggered by one small word "No". Upon hearing this entire tables are cleared in a single swoop, ear piercing screams can be heard for miles (at least I think), and a tantrum ensues. A "time out" usually follows after which my sweet boy returns with a hug, kiss, and "I sorry". Ahh the joys of being two but I wouldn't trade my sweet boy or his alter ego for the world. For every tantrum I get 100 kisses in return. For every broken knick knack I get 200 hugs and a heart filled with love for you!

Materials

Photos: 5 x 7-inch, 4 x 5-inch	Printable transparencies	Sewing machine with white thread	3 (½-inch) adhesive foam dots
Blue/green/yellow/white printed papers: light blue polka dots, pale green polka dots, stripes	1-inch white "b" rub-on transfer	Die-cutting machine	Paper adhesive
	Craft paints: light blue, light green	Dies: 4 x 4⅞-inch frame, ¾-inch "2"	Computer with fonts of your choice
	Mini brads: 2 white, 1 light green	Paintbrush	Printer
		½-inch circle punch	

TODDLER'S RULES

DESIGN BY SHERRY WRIGHT

If you've ever spent time around a 2-year-old, you know who rules the house!

Lay transparency over feature photo with right edge of transparency ¼ inch from right edge of photo. Note position of photo elements that should remain unobstructed; use computer to generate phrases— "Toddler's Rules," "mine.," "If I like it, it's mine.," "If it's in my hand, it's mine.," etc.—randomly over remaining surface of transparency.

Adhere a 12 x 6-inch rectangle of striped paper to bottom of a 12-inch square of light blue polka-dot paper, edges even. Machine-stitch several wavy free-form lines across top edge of striped paper using a straight stitch. Center and adhere a 5 x 7-inch photo to layout 1⅜ inches from top edge of layout; adhere a 4 x 5-inch photo to lower right corner.

Die-cut frame from another piece of transparency. Machine-stitch around center of frame using zigzag stitch. Punch six ½-inch circles from striped paper; mount three on dimensional foam dots. Adhere all circles to transparency frame; adhere frame over smaller photo.

Cut large "2" from light green polka-dot paper; adhere to layout in upper left corner, overlapping larger photo. Adhere "Toddler's Rules" transparency above feature photo.

Paint one bookplate light green and the other light blue. Attach white mini brads to light green bookplate and light green mini brad to right hole of light blue bookplate.

Adhere an 8½-inch piece of striped ribbon across bottom of layout ¾ inch from bottom edge, wrapping left end over left edge and securing on reverse side, and threading right end through light blue bookplate; adhere bookplate and ribbon to layout. Die-cut "2" from a small piece of striped paper; adhere outline of die-cut image inside bookplate.

Adhere a 3½-inch piece of ribbon near upper right corner of layout ½ inch from top edge, wrapping right end over right edge and securing on reverse side. Frame "b" rub-on transfer inside light green bookplate; adhere both over left end of ribbon.

Use computer to generate journaling on another transparency to fit within an area approximately 3½ x 5 inches; trim and adhere journaling to upper right corner of layout, just to right of feature photo. ■

SOURCES: Printed paper from Urban Lily; transparencies from 3M; rub-on transfer from me & my BIG ideas; bookplates and mini brads from Making Memories; ribbon from KI Memories; die-cutting machine and dies from Ellison/Sizzix; adhesive from Beacon.

ONE FINE DAY

DESIGN BY LINDA BEESON

Groups of index-size photos form design elements in this layout of a special family trip.

Ink edges of an 11½-inch square of printed paper with brown ink; adhere to 12-inch square of brown card stock, positioning paper toward bottom left corner a scant ¹⁄₁₆ inch from bottom and left edges. Round off upper right corner of a 10¾ x 11½-inch rectangle of kraft card stock using small plate or bowl for template; ink edges and adhere card stock to layout ¼ inch from left edge and ⅛ inch from bottom edge. Machine-stitch along curve of kraft card stock using zigzag stitch; machine-stitch across bottom near edge of kraft card stock using a straight stitch.

Adhere larger photo to light green card stock and trim, leaving ⅛-inch borders. Adhere photo to lower right corner of layout, ⅝ inch from bottom edge and 1⅛ inches from right edge. Adhere transparent stickers to spell "ZOO" to lower left corner of layout as shown.

Ink edges of index photos with black ink; arrange in groups on upper portion of layout. Adhere. Apply desired words, phrases and year using rub-on transfers; affix brad through upper right corner of layout. ■

SOURCES: Printed paper from BasicGrey; chalk ink pad from Clearsnap Inc.; pigment ink from Tsukineko; stickers from Mustard Moon; rub-on transfers from Making Memories and 7gypsies.

Materials

Color photos: 5¾ x 4³⁄₈ inches, 15–17 index size (approximately 1¼ x ⁷⁄₈ inch and ⁷⁄₈ x 1¼ inches)

Card stock: brown, kraft, light green
Green/white printed paper
Ink pads: brown chalk, black pigment

2-inch transparent black alphabet stickers to spell "ZOO"
Black rub-on transfers: words, phrases
Orange brad

Sewing machine with dark brown thread
Paper adhesive

LEARNING TO SKATE

DESIGN BY TAMI MAYBERRY

A series of photos tell the story of a newly learned skill (with Dad's help, of course!).

Left page: Sand edges of a 1½ x 3½-inch rectangle of blue card stock; adhere to top left corner of an 8½ x 11-inch piece of tan card stock, ¼ inch from left edge and ⅛ inch from top edge. Adhere a 2½ x 3¼-inch photo to layout ¼ inch from blue rectangle and top edge.

Cut an 8-inch circle from circles printed paper; cut into two pieces, cutting through circle vertically 2½ inches from left edge. Adhere smaller section to layout 1 inch from top edge and right edges even. Adhere an 8½ x 4-inch rectangle of striped paper across center of layout, left edges even and right edge overlapping circle. Center and adhere an 8½ x 3¼-inch rectangle of blue card stock to striped rectangle. Adhere a 2½ x 3¼-inch photo to blue card-stock rectangle 1¼ inches from right edge of layout.

Adhere a 2½ x 3¼-inch photo to lower left corner of layout. Adhere a ½-inch-wide strip of blue card stock and a ¾-inch-wide strip of surfboards printed paper across bottom of layout with left ends even with photo; trim right ends of strips even with right edge of layout.

Adhere a 2 x ¼-inch strip of surfboards paper to blue card stock; trim, leaving narrow borders along top and bottom edges and trimming ends even. Adhere to top right corner of layout ¼ inch from top and right edges

even. Attach orange and dark blue mini brads to tan card stock at left end of strip.

Cut the 5 x 7-inch photo into two pieces, cutting through photo vertically 1 inch from left edge. Adhere smaller portion of photo to layout inside partial circle with right edges even; using teal mini brad, attach teal photo turn over edge of photo near upper left corner.

Lightly sand gold alphabet stickers; adhere stickers to spell name on blue rectangle in upper left corner of layout; adhere stickers to spell title on blue rectangle in center of layout.

Right page: Align left page side by side with a second 8½ x 11-inch piece of tan card stock for right page. Adhere remaining portion of printed-paper circle to right page so that it aligns with partial circle on left page. Adhere an 8½ x 4-inch rectangle of striped paper across center of page over circle so that top and bottom edges align with top and bottom edges of matching strip on left page. Center and adhere an 8½ x 3¼-inch rectangle of blue card stock to striped rectangle. Center and adhere a 6 x ¾-inch strip of circles printed paper to blue card stock. Lightly sand edges of a 2¾-inch circle of blue card

CONTINUED ON PAGE 171

Materials

Color photos: 5 x 7-inch, 5 (2½ x 3¼-inch)	printed papers: circles, stripes, surfboards	Mini brads: 2 teal, 2 dark blue, 2 orange	Sandpaper
Card stock: blue, tan	1-inch gold card-stock alphabet and numeral stickers	2 teal photo turns	Paper adhesive
Teal/orange/beige/white/blue		Circle cutter	

Materials

Color photos: 9 x 5¼-inch, 3¼ x 6-inch

Pink/orange/white striped reversible printed card stock

Solid-color card stock: orange, pink

Card stock stickers

1½- to 1¾-inch alphabet foam stamps

Craft paints: pink, orange

Black fine-tip pen (optional)

¼-inch-wide satin grosgrain ribbons: pink, orange

Die-cutting machine with ¾-inch alphabet dies

Corner rounder punch

Stapler with staples

Double-sided tape

Computer with font of your choice

Printer

THE FAIR

DESIGN BY STEPHANIE BARNARD

Bright striped paper in colors to complement your main photo adds festive flair to this fun layout.

Project note: Adhere elements using double-sided tape unless instructed otherwise.

Round off corners of a 12-inch square of striped card stock. Round off upper left corner of larger photo; adhere to striped card stock 2½ inches from top edge with right edges even, leaving left edge and bottom left edge of photo open.

Cut four 1½ x 2-inch rectangles from pink card stock and one from orange card stock; round off corners. Using die-cutting machine and alphabet dies, die-cut letters to spell "the" from pink card stock and adhere to orange rectangle. Using paints as ink, stamp pink rectangles with letters to spell "fair," using pink paint for "f" and orange paint for remaining letters. Adhere die-cut "the" in upper left corner of layout; arrange stamped rectangles to spell "fair" across top of layout.

Round off upper right and lower left corners of smaller photo; adhere to lower left corner of layout, edges even. Round off bottom corners of a 3⅛ x 1½-inch pink card-stock rectangle; tuck straight edge of rectangle up under bottom left edge of larger photo and adhere to layout 1 inch to right of smaller photo. Adhere sticker to visible portion of pink card stock.

Cut a ⅞-inch square of reversible card stock; round off corners on one end. Adhere straight edge, with reverse side up, to the upper left side of a 3½ x 2-inch card-stock sticker with edges even. Adhere sticker to lower right corner of layout ⅜ inch from bottom and right edges.

Cut four 1 x 2-inch rectangles of orange card stock; round off one end of each. Adhere one rectangle to upper right corner of layout ¾ inch from right edge with straight edges even. Adhere remaining strips to bottom of layout 3/16 inch apart, ⅜ inch to right of smaller photo.

Tag: Use computer to generate, or hand-print, journaling on pink card stock to fit within area approximately 2⅛ x 5 inches. Trim card stock to 2⅜ x 5½ inches, positioning journaling at bottom. Round off corners. Cut a 2⅜ x 2-inch rectangle from reversible card stock; turn reverse side up. Round off upper corners. Adhere printed tag to smaller piece, leaving ⅜ inch of smaller tag visible at top. Fold 4-inch lengths of orange and pink ribbon in half; trim ends at an angle and staple folds to top of tag. Tuck tag behind larger photo, sliding it under open left edge. ■

SOURCES: Printed card stock and card-stock stickers from The Paper Loft; die-cutting machine and dies from Ellison/Sizzix; tape from Therm O Web.

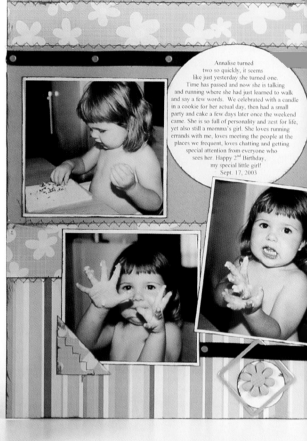

Materials

Color photos: 4¾ x 4-inch, 5 ranging in size from 2¾ x 2½ inches to 3¾ inches square

Card stock: dark pink, white

Printed papers: pink/orange/lavender stripes, orange floral

⅜-inch alphabet stamps

Inks: brown, black

½-inch black alphabet rub-on transfers

2 (1½-inch) square metal-rim tags

8 pink mini brads

2 (⅞-inch) pink flower buttons

³⁄₁₆-inch-wide black grosgrain ribbon

1-inch circle punch

Circle cutter

Craft knife and mat

Craft nippers

Sewing machine with brown thread

Paper adhesive

Craft cement

Computer with fonts of your choice

Printer

BLOW OUT
YOUR CANDLE

DESIGN BY KRISTEN SWAIN

Matted photos and pastel shades
set the stage for a birthday celebration.

Project notes: Ink edges of all photos, paper and cardstock elements with brown ink. *Adhere elements using paper adhesive unless instructed otherwise.*

Left page: Adhere an 8½ x 3¾ rectangle of striped paper across bottom of an 8½ x 11-inch sheet of pink card stock with edges even. Adhere an 8½ x 1½-inch strip of orange floral paper across card stock along top edge of striped paper.

Adhere largest photo to striped paper and trim, leaving ¼-inch borders; adhere to white card stock and trim, leaving ⅛-inch border. Machine-stitch around striped paper border of largest photo using straight stitch. Machine-stitch over edges of orange floral strip using zigzag stitch.

Adhere a ½ x 6-inch strip of striped paper to upper left quadrant of layout ¾ inch from left edge with top edges even. Apply alphabet rub-on transfers to strip to read "blow out your." Use computer to generate 1¼-inch letters to spell "Candle"; print outline of letters only onto white card stock. Cut out individual letters using craft knife and adhere to layout just to right of striped strip.

Using craft knife, cut a 3-inch file folder tab shape from orange paper; stamp caption on tab using brown ink and adhere tab to upper right edge of main photo. Adhere main photo to upper right quadrant of layout ³⁄₁₆ inch from right edge. Cut a 1½-inch square of orange floral paper in half diagonally to form two

photo-mounting corners; machine-stitch over photo-mounting corners using zigzag stitch. Adhere one over upper left corner of photo (remaining corner will be used on right page).

Adhere two smaller photos to white card stock and trim, leaving ⅛-inch borders; adhere to lower portion of layout. Adhere 1-inch white card-stock circle to layout 2⅝ inches from right edge and overlapping seam between orange floral and striped papers. Snap shank off button; adhere to card-stock circle using craft cement. Tear paper from center of one metal-rim tag; thread rim onto ribbon. Adhere ribbon across layout from right edge to edge of photo, ⅛ inch from top edge of orange floral strip, positioning tag over circle and button. Adhere tag to layout and attach mini brads through ends of ribbon.

Right page: Adhere an 8½ x 3¾ rectangle of striped paper across bottom of an 8½ x 11-inch sheet of pink card stock with edges even. Adhere an 8½ x 1½-inch strip of orange floral paper across card stock along top edge of striped paper. Adhere an 8½ x 1¼-inch strip of orange floral paper across layout ⅛ inch from top edge. Zigzag-stitch across top and bottom of orange floral strips.

Adhere ribbon across layout ⅛ inch below bottom edge of top orange floral strip. Use computer to generate journaling to fit within a 3¾- to 4-inch circle; print out

CONTINUED ON PAGE 168

learning to write

learning to write

W

TRACE WRITE LEARN TRACE WRITE LEARN

a New beginning

Tracing the dots, learning those fine motor skills, on her way towards learning to write. Annalise has been drawing just fine now for a while, making circles and now figures with faces and arms and legs, but this is the beginning, tracing the lines, moving her hand in a specific pattern, and making lines that will eventually lead to letters and numbers, then moving on to words and sentences. I love the way she grips the pencil with those little precious fingers, holding on and pushing down hard, being sure to leave her mark where her pencil goes. 2004

Materials

Color photos: 6 x 4-inch, 4½ x
   3⅜-inch, 5¼ x 3½-inch

Red card stock

Printed papers: apples, off-white
   with red polka dots, green
   with blue pin dots

Printable transparency

9 kraft photo corners

Black ink

⅝-inch flat button

4 red brads

1¾-inch red silk daisy

⁷⁄₁₆-inch-wide deep pink/white
   pin-dot ribbon

Label maker with black tape

Circle template

Craft knife

Paper adhesive

Craft cement

Computer with fonts of
   your choice

Printer

A NEW BEGINNING

DESIGN BY KRISTEN SWAIN

Give life's little milestones new significance with journaling on a scrapbook page.

Project note: Adhere elements using paper adhesive unless instructed otherwise.

Adhere a 3¼ x 12-inch strip of apples paper to left side of a 12-inch-square of red card stock with edges even. Ink edges of an 8¾ x 10½-inch piece of polka-dot paper; center and adhere to layout against edge of apples paper strip. Ink edges of a 9 x 6½-inch piece of pin-dot paper and adhere in lower right portion of layout with right edges even and overlapping polka-dot paper.

Use computer to generate "New", using 2-inch letters in desired font, and journaling to fit within an area measuring 5 x 4⅜ inches. Print onto transparency; trim and adhere to layout over pin-dot paper.

Ink edges of 12 x ¾-inch strips of polka-dot and pin-dot papers. Adhere polka-dot strip across layout ½ inch from bottom edge; adhere pin-dot strip across layout ½ inch from top edge. Attach red brads at ends of strips.

Ink edges of a 6 x 1¼-inch strip of apples paper, showing a row of apples. Adhere near bottom of layout 1 inch from right edge and overlapping horizontal polka-dot strip by ⅜ inch.

Attach photo corners to all four corners of 6 x 4-inch and 5¼ x 3½-inch photos; attach corner to top left corner of remaining photo. Adhere photos to red card stock and trim, leaving ⅛-inch borders. Use computer to print "learning to write" in a circle to fit within a 2⅜-inch circle; print out onto red card stock and trim 2⅜-inch circle around words; ink edges. Adhere photos and "learning to write" embellishment to layout as shown.

Print "Trace Write Learn" or other words repeatedly on black label tape; trim to fit along left side of layout between horizontal pin-dot strip and top edge of bottom photo. Adhere to layout ½ inch from left edge.

Use computer to print outlines only of "a" and "beginning" in script-style font onto red card stock; cut out using craft knife and adhere to layout overlapping "New" as shown. Tie knot in center of a 2-inch piece of ribbon and trim ends; adhere to button using craft cement. Adhere button to silk daisy using craft cement; adhere daisy to lower right corner of main photo using craft cement. ∎

SOURCES: Printed papers from Daisy D's Paper Co., Die Cuts With A View and Making Memories; transparency from 3M; photo corners from Canson; brads from Making Memories; ribbon from Li'l Davis Designs; label maker and tape from DYMO Corp.

BELIEVE

DESIGN BY STEPHANIE BARNARD

Relive the days when you still believed in the magic of Santa with large photos on a two-page spread.

Project note: Adhere photos and card-stock elements using double-sided tape; adhere remaining elements using adhesive dots or craft cement as indicated.

Right page: Tear across top edge of a 12 x 5½-inch strip of solid red card stock; adhere across bottom of 12-inch square of Christmas printed card stock with right, left and bottom edges even. Machine-stitch across strip near torn edge using a straight stitch. Cut two 1¼-inch squares of green card stock; adhere one to right edge of torn strip 2¼ inches from bottom, with right edges even. Adhere second to bottom edge of torn strip 1¾ inches from left edge, with bottom edges even. Center and adhere two 5¾ x 4-inch photos to torn strip as shown.

Tear a 1½-inch square of solid red card stock in half diagonally. Adhere one half to upper right corner of layout, matching straight edges. Machine-stitch along torn edge using a straight stitch.

Adhere 6 x 4-inch photo to a 6⅝ x 3½-inch rectangle of green card stock ½ inch from top edge and ⅝ inch from right edge. Clip red paper clip over top edge of photo panel ¾ inch from right edge; hand-stitch charm to lower right corner of green card stock. Adhere photo panel to layout ⅞ inch from right edge and 1¼ inches from top edge.

Use computer to generate, or hand-print, journaling on red die-cut tag; adhere to solid green card stock and trim, leaving very narrow borders. Punch hole in top of tag. Thread a 3¾-inch piece of ribbon through hole in tag; secure with staple, attaching charm. Adhere tag and ribbon to upper left corner of layout.

Left page: Tear down right edge of a 2 x 12-inch strip solid red card stock; adhere down left side of 12-inch square of Christmas printed card stock with top, left and bottom edges even. Machine-stitch down strip near torn edge using a straight stitch. Adhere ribbon to torn strip ⅝ inch from left edge of layout; staple ribbon near ends. Adhere three evenly spaced charms down ribbon using craft cement.

Center and adhere photo to a 7½ x 5½-inch rectangle of solid red card stock. Machine-stitch around photo on card stock, alternating between straight stitch and a wide zigzag stitch. Clip green paper clip over top edge of card stock 1 inch from left edge. Adhere photo panel to green card stock and trim, leaving ³⁄₁₆-inch borders. Pierce lower right corner of photo panel with stick pin; tie ribbon in bow around stick pin. Adhere photo panel to layout 1½ inches from right edge and 1¾ inches from top edge.

Cut 1⅞ x 2⅜-inch and 1¾ x 1⅛-inch rectangles from solid red card stock; ink edges with distress ink. Die-cut letters from green card stock to spell "believe"; adhere "b" to larger red rectangle and "v" to smaller red rectangle. Adhere letters across bottom of layout. ∎

SOURCES: Printed card stock, paper clips and metal embellishments from Around the Block Products; die-cutting machine and dies from Ellison/Sizzix; ribbon from Creative Impressions; tape and adhesive dots from Therm O Web.

Materials

Color photos: 2 (6 x 4-inch),
  2 (5½ x 4-inch)

Red Christmas-themed
  reversible printed card stock

Solid-color card stock: red, green

Distress ink

Black fine-tip marker (optional)

Red-with-green-stitches ¼-inch-
  wide ribbon

Plastic Christmas paper clips:
  red, green

Pewter-finish Christmas-themed
  metal embellishments:
  5 charms, stick pin

Die-cutting machine

Die cuts: 2½ x 4⅞-inch tag, 2-
  inch letters

Stapler with staples

¼-inch hole punch

Dark gray thread

Hand-sewing needle

Sewing machine

Double-sided tape

Adhesive dots

Craft cement

Computer with font of
  your choice

Printer

SLUGGER

DESIGN BY LINDA BEESON

Red rickrack and black label tape border a series of closely cropped photos of a special event.

"Slugger": Using word-processing program, type "SLUGGER" in ¾-inch letters; fill in text box with black and fill in letters with white; print onto white card stock and trim to 1½ x 4 inches.

"#1 Athlete" panel: Using word-processing program, type "#1 Athlete," name and other words using desired fonts, leaving a blank area in the upper right corner that will be filled later by the laser-cut initial tag. Fill in the text box with black; fill some words with red, leaving the others white. Size to 4 x 1¼ inches and print; trim. Adhere laser-cut circle initial tag to red card stock; trim, leaving a very narrow border. Adhere tag to upper right area of panel.

Use computer to generate journaling as desired in upper right area of a 12-inch-square sheet of white card stock. Adhere three circles punched from black card stock to embellish title as shown. Print smaller photos (photos on sample project measure 1⅝ x 2¹⁵⁄₁₆ inches); sand edges lightly and adhere photos to card stock below journaling. Stamp date on lower right corner of layout. Machine-stitch rickrack to card stock below photos using a zigzag stitch.

Print featured photo to desired size (on sample, it measures 4 x 9¼ inches); sand edges lightly and adhere to layout to left of journaling. Adhere "Slugger" and "#1 Athlete" panels to layout above and below featured photo. Adhere printed paper to cover remaining card stock along left edge. Print "Hey Batter Batter" on label tape; adhere over seam between featured photo and printed paper. ■

SOURCES: Printed paper from Scrappin Sports & More; circle tag from EZ Laser Designs; date stamp from Making Memories; label maker and tape from DYMO Corp.

Tip: If you don't have a wide-format printer, you can still print journaling directly onto the background of your layout. Cut a 3½-inch-wide strip off the left edge of the 12-inch-square sheet of white card stock. Print the journaling in the correct position on the 8½-inch-wide sheet. Then reassemble your 12-inch-square layout base by laying the printed piece and the cut-off strip side by side, facedown. Adhere a 2-inch-wide strip of paper over the seam to splice the pieces together.

Materials

Digital photos	1-inch round black laser-cut	Fine sandpaper	Paper adhesive
Photo paper	initial tag	Sewing machine with black	Computer with fonts of
Card stock: black, red, white	Date stamp	thread	your choice
Baseball-themed printed paper	Black ink pad	Label maker with black tape	Wide-format printer
	Red jumbo rickrack	⁵⁄₁₆-inch hole punch	

SLUGGER

HEY BATTER BATTER, HEY BATTER BATTER, HEY BATTER BATTER, HEY BATTER BATTER

Play Ball

#1 ATHLETE

RILEY

DREAM PASSION

It's all in the game

HOmerun

r

EXPLORE

RILEY IS UP TO BAT

NO runners on base
NO strikes
NO balls
NO innings
Just big, plastic, colorful
balls and a big orange bat.
Riley is up to bat!

Grandpa was pitching balls to Shantel and
Cody for batting practice. Riley is 2 1/2
years old, but he believes he is able to
do anything the other kids can do.   Of
course, he wanted his turn to bat. It was
pretty cute to watch him try to hold the
bat just right and stand just right and
swing the bat just right, according to how
Grandpa instructed him. He thought he was
occasionally hitting the ball, but it was
really Grandpa hitting the bat with the
balls when he threw them.

February 2005

w•h•y ?

Why must you whistle
ALL THE TIME?

No, seriously! From dawn until
you fall asleep, you are always
whistling!

Crazy

Dane 04/06

whistler

WHISTLER

DESIGN BY RACHAEL GIALLONGO

Endearing, annoying or downright mystifying—the strange habits of loved ones can help define a personality!

Project note: Adhere photo, card stock and paper using paper adhesive. Adhere remaining elements using craft glue.

Ink all chipboard embellishments with distress ink.

Round off upper corners and tear bottom edge off an 11 x 8½-inch piece of pin-dot printed paper; center and adhere to a 12-inch square of beige card stock ½ inch from top and side edges.

Adhere a 5½ x 6½-inch piece of cork paper to upper right corner of printed paper, 1 inch from top and right edges of layout. Adhere a 7 x 5-inch piece of tan card stock to printed paper, overlapping cork paper, 2 inches from top edge and 1 inch from left edge of layout. Adhere photo to cork paper ½ inch from top, right and bottom edges of cork paper.

Add journaling to ½-inch-high strips of gold card stock; adhere to tan card stock as shown. Apply rub-on transfer next to one line of journaling. Adhere "why"

chipboard letters, decorative brads and chipboard question mark as shown. Adhere ribbon across layout ½ inch above torn edge of printed paper; wrap ends over edge to reverse side and adhere. Layer initial and personality stickers onto chipboard oval; adhere oval over ribbon 1⅛ inches from left edge of layout as shown.

Round off corners on an 11 x 2¼-inch rectangle of dark brown card stock. Lay out round chipboard alphabet for title; mark overlapping areas with a pencil and cut off using a craft knife. Fit round letters onto dark brown card-stock strip; adhere. Paint center of each letter with clear-drying glue; sprinkle with microbeads and tap off excess. Add name and date below ribbon near right edge using fine-tip marker. ∎

SOURCES: Printed paper from My Mind's Eye; cork paper from Creative Impressions; round chipboard alphabet from Heidi Swapp; chipboard monogram from BasicGrey; monogram stickers from Creative Imaginations; rub-on transfer from Maisy Mo Designs; brads from American Traditional Designs.

Materials

4 x 6-inch color photo	1¾-inch-diameter round	Black fine-tip marker	Pencil
Card stock: beige, tan, dark	alphabet, 2½ x 2¾-inch	1-inch black arrow	Craft knife
brown, gold	oval monogram, 4-inch	rub-on transfer	Paintbrush
Turquoise with beige pin dots	question mark	2 round brass decorative brads	Paper adhesive
printed paper	Stickers: monogram,	Microbeads: green, gold	Clear-drying craft glue
Cork paper	personality word	⁷⁄₁₆-inch-wide dark brown	
Chipboard embellishments:	Distress ink	grosgrain ribbon	

BEACHCOMBER

DESIGN BY MANDY KOONTZ

This digital layout combines bright colors, bits of journaling and a black-and-white photo to create an energetic and lively layout.

Open new document within Photoshop. Adjust settings: width and height: 12 inches; 300 dpi resolution; color mode: RGB; background contents: transparent.

Background: Open "Backs" folder in Tropical Breezes kit; open "palmtrees2" background. Remove orange color from background by selecting Eyedropper tool and clicking on solid-orange area of background. Select Paint Bucket tool and click on this newly transparent document. Background should now be filled in with a solid version of color on printed paper.

Open digital photo; crop and resize as desired, then position photo on layout. ***Note:*** *To resize your photo using the Free Transform feature, click "Edit," "Free Transform." While pressing Shift key, click and drag on corner of photo to alter its size. To secure the photo in its desired size, click the "Commit Transform" (checkmark) button at top of Photoshop browser.*

In "layers" palette, double-click on layer containing your photo. When layers style box opens, select Drop Shadows; close. From this point on, you will add a drop shadow to every paper or element layer on your layout.

Open "Backs" folder in digital kit; open "dots1" background. Select Rectangle Marquee tool from toolbox; click and drag to form a square. ***Note:*** *If you prefer a perfect square, press Shift while dragging tool. Select Move tool from toolbar; click and drag selection to layout.*

Your paper layer will probably be on top of the photo at this point. To move it behind photo, press Ctrl on keyboard, then press "[." Repeat with printed papers labeled "dots2," "back3" and "palmtrees1." ***Note:*** *Use the*

"Free Transform" method described previously to resize the paper layers as desired. To rotate a paper, make sure that the layer on which it rests is selected in the layers palette; go to "Edit," "Transform," then "Rotate." The selected paper can now be rotated as desired.

Add a large strip of patterned paper across bottom of layout: Open "Backs" folder and select "back1." Using Rectangle Marquee tool, select rectangular portion of paper, taking care to stretch selection from one side to the other; this ensures that the selected paper will cover your layout from side to side. Select Move tool from toolbox; click and drag your selection to position it at bottom of layout.

Browse to kit folder; open "elements" folder and select "definition." Use Move tool to drag definition label to your layout; position it beneath the photo. ***Note:*** *If this layer becomes hidden, simultaneously click "Ctrl" and "]" as often as needed to bring it to the top.*

Within "elements" folder, open the "straight pins" folder; select "blank" straight pin and drag it to your layout. With straight pin on top layer, place it on your definition label. Click Erase tool from toolbox and using small, hard, round brush, erase section of the straight pin so that it appears to have pierced the definition label.

Within "elements" folder, open the "ribbons" folder; select the "dots" ribbon and drag it to your layout. Place left edge of ribbon on left edge of the head of the blank straight pin. The ribbon should fit perfectly against edge of straight pin so that it appears to have been wrapped around the edge.

CONTINUED ON PAGE 169

May 2006

Par*a*dise
* Place of ideal beauty or loveliness
* A state of delight

I thought Allyson might really love the water. But I've found that she really loves the sand even more. She'll play in the waves for a short while, but then she always goes back to the sand and the shells

BEACH
comber

Materials

Digital photo

Glossy-finish photo paper

Digital printed paper and elements

Digital brush programs

Computer with photo-editing and digital-imaging programs

Printer

1. Wait and wait and wait until it snows.
2. Wait some more.
3. When it's finally snowing, go make sure it's snowing enough that you might actually catch a snowflake in your mouth.
4. Lean your head back and open your mouth as wide as possible. Hold your arms out for balance and so that if you lose your balance and fall on your back you can just tell anyone who saw that you were making a snow angel.
5. Big fluffy snowflakes are the best, you can catch them easier and actually feel them on your tongue, if it's not frozen from being out in the cold for so long.
6. Celebrate your success of catching a single drop of frozen water on your frozen tongue by going inside and getting a large drink of water from the cooler.

Materials

Color photos: 5¼ x 4½-inch, 4 x 3-inch, 5¼ x 2⅜-inch,

Card stock: lavender, light lavender, white

Lavender/blue/green printed papers: stripes, blocks

Transparent vellum

2⅞ x ⅜-inch white card-stock tags

Stickers: assorted snowflakes, ¾-inch square snowflake sticker

¼- to ⅜-inch alphabet stamps

Fine-tip black marker

Ink: black, lavender

Alphabet stickers to spell "catch"

½-inch black alphabet rub-on transfers to spell "SNOWFLAKE"

Brads: 5 silver, 3 purple mini

¼-inch rhinestones

1-inch paper clip

Ribbons: ½-inch wide lavender, 7/16-inch-wide lavender, blue, white

Stapler with staples

Paper adhesive

Craft cement

Computer with fonts of your choice

Printer

HOW TO CATCH A SNOWFLAKE

DESIGN BY KRISTEN SWAIN

Creatively cropped photos and a bit of journaling turn an everyday occurrence into something to remember.

Project note: *Adhere elements using paper adhesive unless instructed otherwise.*

Adhere an 11 x 1-inch strip of striped paper across top of an 11 x 8½-inch piece of lavender card stock ¼ inch from top edge. Adhere snowflake stickers to top 6 inches of layout.

Cut an 11 x 3-inch strip from blocks printed paper, trimming around edges of blocks along top edge. Cut three 1 x 1½-inch tags from white card stock; ink edges with lavender; attach purple mini brads to top of tags. Arrange photos, blocks, strip and tags onto layout, positioning feature photo on left side, ⅞ inch from left edge and ¼ inch below striped strip; tuck bottom edge of photo behind blocks strip.

Arrange remaining photos on right side of layout, overlapping blocks strip as shown and tucking tags behind top edge of top photo; adhere photos, blocks, strip and tags to layout. With lavender ink, stamp winter-themed words onto tags. Tuck a tab cut from light lavender card stock behind right edge of feature photo ¾ inch from upper right corner; add journaling to tab with fine-tip marker. Adhere tab to layout.

Use computer to generate, or hand-print, journaling onto vellum to fit within an area measuring 5½ x 2¼ inches; adhere journaling over blocks, strip in lower left corner of layout, 1 inch from bottom edge. Adhere ½-inch-wide lavender ribbon across bottom of layout below journaling; fold up left end at an angle and secure with a staple.

Title: Stamp "how" and "to" onto ⅞ x ⅜-inch tags using black ink; thread tags onto paper clip and clip over top edge of layout in upper left corner. Arrange tags as shown and adhere to layout. Adhere alphabet stickers to silver brads to spell "catch"; attach brads to layout ½ inch to right of paper clip and ¼ inch from top edge of strip. Stamp "A" onto ¾-inch square snowflake sticker; adhere to striped strip to right of brads. Apply rub-on transfers to spell "SNOWFLAKE" near bottom edge of strip.

Tie small bows from lengths of blue, lavender and white ⁷⁄₁₆-inch-wide ribbon; adhere in a row in upper right corner of layout over striped paper strip 1¼ inches from edge. Adhere rhinestones to layout as desired using craft cement. ∎

SOURCES: Printed papers from Karen Foster Design and Paper Adventures; vellum from The Paper Co.; stamps from PSX; stickers from Autumn Leaves and Making Memories; rub-on transfers, brads and brad stickers from Making Memories; ribbons from Offray.

SNOW WONDERFUL

DESIGN BY KRISTEN SWAIN

Shades of cool blue and glittery embellishments set the stage for baby's first snow experience.

Project notes: Adhere card stock and stickers using paper adhesive. Adhere remaining elements using craft glue.

Center and adhere a 3 x 10-inch strip of polka-dot printed paper down left side of a 12-inch square of blue card stock with left edges even; repeat on right side of card stock, adhering a 2¼ x 10-inch strip. Draw a smooth, freehand "wave" across center of a 12 x 3¼-inch strip of striped printed paper with stripes running vertically. Cut paper into two pieces along wave line; adhere one along top of layout and the other along bottom with straight edges even. (Wave shapes will overlap ends of polka-dot strips.)

Adhere a 12 x ¼-inch strip of dark blue card stock across layout ¼ inch from top edge; repeat across bottom. Adhere a 12-inch strip of polka-dot ribbon across top of layout just below dark blue strip.

Adhere photos to white card stock; cut out, leaving narrow borders. Adhere to layout as shown. Center and adhere a 4½-inch circle cut from blue card stock to a 4¾-inch circle cut from dark blue card stock; adhere circles to layout, overlapping corner of center photo.

Tag: Use computer to generate, or hand-print, journaling to fit within an area measuring approximately 2½ x 5 inches. Print journaling onto blue card stock; trim a 2⅝ x 7-inch tag shape around journaling. Adhere tag to layout on right side, 2 inches from top edge and ⅜ inch from right edge.

Tie blue ribbon in a bow to fit at top of tag. Poke white wire through round snowflake sticker and form wire loop so tag dangles from bow; poke wire ends through knot of ribbon bow. Clip excess wire and bend ends under; adhere bow with tag to top of journaling tag. Embellish bottom of tag with round "Winter" and striped stickers. Adhere "Winter Wonderland" sticker over upper left corner of top photo.

Use computer to print outlines of 5¼-inch capital "S" and 1- to 1½-inch letters to complete "now wonderful" onto white card stock. Cut out individual letters using craft knife and adhere to layout as shown. Brush "Snow" letters with clear-drying glue; sprinkle with "ice" crystals.

By hand, lightly draw simple snowflake pattern overlapping upper curve of "S." Punch holes in pattern using a large needle; stitch snowflake through holes using light blue embroidery floss and tapestry needle. Adhere ghost snowflakes and rhinestones to layout as desired. ■

SOURCES: Printed papers and stickers from Bo-Bunny Press; ribbon from May Arts and Craft Supply; ice crystals from Suze Weinberg Design Studio; ghost snowflakes from Heidi Swapp.

Snow Wonderful

Annalise was just four months old when we took her outside to enjoy the first few flakes of the season. I bundled her up in a cuddly snow outfit and Chris and I went outside. I was surprised that she actually looked around, watching the flakes float past her face, fascinated, long before she actually seemed unhappy that her face was getting cold. I love the expression of sheer wonder on her chubby little face. Her first snow experience was snow wonderful!! 1.02

Materials

Color photos: 4 x 6-inch, 3⅜ x 4⅝-inch

Card stock: blue, dark blue, white

Printed papers: pale green/blue/white polka-dots, pale green/blue/white stripes

Card stock stickers: ¾-inch

round winter-themed, blue-and-white stripes

Black fine-tip marker

2½-inch "Winter Wonderland" acrylic sticker

3 transparent ghost snowflakes

Plastic "ice" crystals

Clear rhinestones

White craft wire

Wire nippers

Ribbons: ⅝-inch-wide white with blue polka dots, ⅜-inch-wide light blue

Light blue embroidery floss

Needles: large, tapestry

Paper adhesive

Clear-drying craft glue

Computer with fonts of your choice

Printer

REMEMBER THIS MOMENT

DESIGN BY TAMI MAYBERRY

Turn an impromptu snapshot into a priceless portrait you'll treasure forever.

Project note: Adhere elements using paper adhesive unless instructed otherwise.

Round off upper and lower right corners on a 10 x 7½-inch piece of floral printed paper; ink edges. Adhere printed paper to tan card stock and trim, leaving narrow borders along top, right and bottom edges and trimming left edges even; ink edges of tan card stock. Center and adhere paper/card-stock panel to an 11 x 8½-inch piece of coral card stock, left edges even.

Adhere a 1½ x 7½-inch strip of multicolored striped paper to layout 1½ inches from right edge, aligning top and bottom edges with edges of underlying floral printed paper. Adhere "memories" oval metal tile to bottom of striped strip using craft cement.

Ink edges of a 3½-inch circle of coral striped paper; adhere to tan card stock and trim, leaving narrow border; ink edges of tan card stock. Adhere a 3½ x 1-inch strip of multicolored striped paper horizontally across circle; round short edges to match circle. Apply rub-on transfers to circle: "Remember" above strip; "this moment" below strip; and "ten" centered on strip. Adhere circle to layout 1¼ inches from top edge, overlapping striped strip by ¼ inch.

Center and adhere photo to layout with left edges even. Ink edges of a 4½ x ½-inch strip of multicolored striped paper; adhere strip to layout just above bottom edge of photo and overlapping photo by about 1¼ inches. Apply "Beautiful" rub-on transfer to layout over strip. ∎

SOURCES: Printed paper and rub-on transfers from Scenic Route Paper Co.; metal word tile from Darice.

Materials

5 x 7-inch photo

Card stock: tan, coral

Printed papers: coral floral, coral
  stripe, coral/teal/brown stripe

Brown ink

Black rub-on transfers:
  "Remember this moment,"
  "ten," "Beautiful"

"Memories" oval metal word tile

Corner rounder punch

Paper adhesive

Craft cement

Materials

Color photos: 4⅞ x 4-inch, 2¾ x 2½-inch, 3 ranging in size from 4½ x 3⅜ inches to 3¾ x 3⅜ inches

Card stock: light green, green, light orange, dark orange

⅜- to ¼-inch alphabet stamps

Black ink pad

Black fine-tip marker (optional)

2 sets 1½-inch gold metal spoon and fork charms

4 orange mini brads

Silver alphabet dog tags to spell "FEED"

Orange fiber

1-inch flower punch

Paper adhesive

Craft cement

Computer with font of your choice

Printer

I CAN FEED MYSELF

DESIGN BY KRISTEN SWAIN

Commemorate first attempts—at eating, walking or riding a bike—with lots of photos and a bit of journaling.

Project note: Adhere elements using paper adhesive unless instructed otherwise.

Punched-flower panels: Punch flowers from light orange card stock. Arrange flowers in a tight pattern on shapes cut from green card stock: 1⅝ x 11-inch strip, 2 x 2⅞-inch rectangle, and 2½ x 2¾-inch rectangle. Adhere flowers to card-stock shapes; trim overhanging flowers even with edges. Adhere flower panels to dark orange card stock and trim, leaving 3/16-inch borders along long edges only of strip and ⅛-inch borders around small rectangles.

Left page: Adhere a 6¼ x ½-inch strip of light orange card stock across an 8½ x 11-inch sheet of green card stock ½ inch from bottom edge with right end of strip even with right edge of card stock. Adhere a 6¼ x ½-inch strip of dark orange card stock across layout ½ inch from top edge with right end of strip even with right edge of card stock.

Adhere 1⅝ x 11-inch flower strip down left side of layout, against ends of light orange and dark orange strips. Adhere ¼ x ½-inch pieces of light orange and dark orange on left side of flower strip, lined up with with 6¼-inch strips of each color that are already in place. Adhere largest strip and photo to light orange card stock and trim, leaving ⅛-inch border. Adhere photo to green card stock and trim, leaving ⅛-inch border. Adhere photo to layout 2¾ inches from top edge and ⅛ inch from right edge.

Adhere smallest photo to green card stock and trim, leaving ⅛-inch border. Adhere to layout, slightly overlapping lower left corner of larger photo.

Adhere 2 x 2⅞-inch punched-flower rectangle to lower right corner of layout as shown. String fork and spoon charms on orange fiber; tie in a bow. Adhere charms and bow to punched-flower rectangle using craft cement.

Using mini brads, attach alphabet dog tags to spell "FEED" across top of layout approximately 1⅝ inches from top edge. Stamp "I can" and "myself" to left and right of dog tags respectively.

Right page: Use computer to generate, or hand-print, journaling onto bottom third of an 8½ x 11-inch sheet of light green card stock to fit within an area measuring approximately 7⅜ x 1¼ inches. Print so that journaling begins approximately 2⅝ inches above bottom edge of card stock.

Adhere an 8½ x ½-inch strip of light orange card stock across bottom of layout ⅜ inch from bottom edge. Adhere an 8½ x ½-inch strip of dark orange card stock across top of layout ½ inch from top edge.

Adhere remaining photos to green card stock and trim, leaving ⅛-inch borders. Arrange photos on layout, overlapping as desired, and adhere. Adhere remaining punched flower panel in upper right corner of layout. String remaining charms on orange fiber; tie in a bow. Adhere charms and bow to punched flower rectangle using craft cement. ■

SOURCES: Stamps from PSX; dog tags from Making Memories; fiber and punch from EK Success Ltd.

'50 FORD

September 2005

SIXTY-SIX

'50 FORD

DESIGN BY SUSAN STRINGFELLOW

Clear, crisp photos and vintage-look papers combine in this stunning layout design. A special pocket holds journaling tags.

Adhere a 10 x 6½-inch piece of burgundy dot paper in upper right corner of a 12-inch square of light brown printed paper as shown. Center and adhere a 6¾-inch piece of ribbon down right side of burgundy dot paper near right edge. Adhere a 1⅞ x 1½-inch piece of gold paper to upper left corner of layout near top edge with left edges even. Machine-stitch around edges of burgundy dot paper, over ribbon ends, and across bottom of layout ¼ inch from edge using a straight stitch and black thread.

Adhere largest photo to tan card stock and cut out, leaving ⅛-inch borders along top and sides and ¼-inch border across bottom; center and adhere top, left and bottom edges of photo to burgundy dot paper, leaving right edge open for tags. Stamp decorative designs and "Memories" along left edge of layout. Using pattern provided (page 170), cut a flourish from brown paper; adhere down left side of layout, overlapping largest photo as shown. Before securing bottom portion of flourish, center and adhere 6 x 4-inch photo to layout just above stitching at bottom, tucking left edge behind overlapping curl of flourish as shown; finish adhering flourish.

Adhere 2⅞ x 4-inch photo to black card stock and cut out, leaving ⅛-inch borders. Machine-stitch around photo ⅛ inch from edge using a straight stitch and black thread. Attach mini brads in corners. Adhere photo at an angle to lower right corner of layout, overlapping 6 x 4-inch photo.

Stamp "50" on gold paper; cut out, leaving ⅛-inch borders, and adhere to layout near left edge and overlapping largest photo. Tuck left end of a 7¾-inch piece of brown trim under zero in "50" and adhere trim across bottom of largest photo. Stamp "Ford" on layout after "50," overlapping bottom of burgundy dot rectangle.

Attach two 2-inch lengths of ribbon to buckle using regular brads. Adhere ribbons and buckle toward lower left corner of layout as shown, overlapping edge of 6 x 4-inch photo.

Tags: Use computer to generate journaling onto light brown printed paper to fit within two areas measuring 7 x 2½ inches. Print out; trim to size and adhere to black card stock. Cut out, leaving narrow borders. Machine-stitch around edges of tags using a straight stitch and black thread. Stitch trim and/or buttons down right edge of tags; tuck tags behind main photo under right edge. ■

SOURCES: Printed paper and ribbons from BasicGrey; stamps from Sugarloaf Products; brads from Making Memories; buckle from Paper Studio.

PATTERN ON PAGE 170

Materials

Color photos: 7⅛ x 5⅝-inch, 6 x 4-inch, 2⅞ x 4-inch
Card stock: tan, black
Printed papers: burgundy dot, light brown, brown, gold
Stamps: decorative images, "Memories," 2-inch numerals, 1-inch alphabet
Black ink pad
¾-inch-wide tan/gold/green woven ribbon
Fabric trims: brown, green/beige
4 small buttons
Brass brads: 2 regular, 4 mini
½ x 1-inch brass buckle
Craft knife
Sewing machine with black thread
Permanent double-sided adhesive
Computer with printer

But they are just daffodils, you say?

I know that's what they look like to you, but I see so much more.
You know how they refer to COMFORT FOOD?
Well, I think these are my COMFORT FLOWERS, if there is such a thing.
I look at them and they generate good memories. As we get older we must become nostalgic, that thing that makes us think about our past, even back to our childhood. We remember things or events that make us smile, that bring a kind of COMFORT.

Like Rocky Road ice cream, for instance. When my sister and I were young, my dad took us to an old Carnation ice cream parlor a few times where there were stools and they hand dipped cones with several choices of flavors and my choice would be Rocky Road.
I loved the marshmallows in it. I had pretty much forgotten about those occasions until the last few years and so I seem to have a renewed interest in Rocky Road ice cream/ That's the same kind of a deal with Daffodils. The last couple years, come spring, I am intrigued with Daffodils.
In fact, I finally planted some bulbs last year. You don't see alot of these in Southern California.
Daffodils were a part of my growing up years. I was born and raised in Tacoma and while I really didn't "get" the significance of these yellow flowers back then, that area was known for it's Daffodil fields. We had the Daffodil parade with Daffodil floats. Our high schools had Daffodil princesses and one would become the Daffodil queen. In the surrounding cities, we had fields and fields of swaying Daffodils.
It was later in life that I would realize that every year Pasadena, CA had roses and a rose parade. Oxnard, CA has it's strawberries and a strawberry festival. Gilroy, CA has a garlic festival. Carpinteria has an Avocado festival and on and on across the country. These are vital parts of these cities and the celebrations around Daffodils was an vital part of the area where I was raised, something I would only realize the significance of these many years later.
Have I said I LOVE Daffodils?

comfort flowers

DAFFODILS
10 Stem Field
2005
"Grown in USA"

"Sometimes I arrive with my buds closed; other times my blooms have already opened. In either case, if you cut 1/2 inch off my stem and place me

COMFORT FLOWERS

DESIGN BY LINDA BEESON

Journal your feelings about your favorite comfort item and leave a lasting legacy for your loved ones.

Plan placement of photo. Working within word-processing program, type journaling to fit within an area measuring 6½ x 9½ inches, wrapping text around area reserved for photo. Add border around journaling if desired. Center and print journaling onto an 8¼ x 10¾-inch piece of gray card stock. Center and adhere journaling to an 8½ x 11-inch piece of black card stock. Adhere plastic identification tab down right-hand margin of layout with top edge even with top of journaling block.

Working within photo-editing software, size photo to fit in allotted space, allowing room for ⅛-inch borders. Type "comfort flowers" in white ¾-inch letters up left edge of photo. Print photo and adhere to black card stock; trim, leaving ⅛-inch borders. Adhere photo to layout.

Print three postage stamp–sized photos; adhere one in upper left corner of journaling block and two in lower right corner of layout. ■

SOURCE: Photo paper from Epson.

Materials

Digital photos	Double-sided matte	Plastic identification tab	Computer with photo-editing
Card stock: gray, black	photo paper	from bouquet	software
			Printer

BEST SURPRISE EVER

DESIGN BY KATHLEEN PANEITZ

Things can be just as important to us as people, places or events, so make sure to include favorite objects in your scrapbooks.

Project notes: Adhere paper elements with paper adhesive; adhere remaining elements with permanent adhesive.

Adhere a 6½ x 9½-inch piece of light green/pink printed paper to a 12-inch square of yellow card stock with top edges even and ⅝ inch from left edge. Adhere a 12 x 1¼-inch strip of blue printed paper across card stock 1¼ inches from bottom edge. Adhere a 2 x 3-inch strip of blue printed paper to top right corner of layout with top edges even and ⅞ inch from right edge of card stock. Adhere larger image to layout ⅜ inch from left edge and ⅝ inch from top edge.

Adhere smaller photo to white card stock; cut out, leaving very narrow border. Affix hinge to top edge of photo and adhere hinge to layout over larger image using accompanying mini brads, positioning hinge 6⅛ inches from top edge and 2¼ inches from right edge.

Adhere velvety stickers to spell "Best" along bottom edge of larger photo. Apply alphabet rub-on transfers to spell "surprise" in margin of green paper below larger photo. Apply alphabet rub-on transfers to spell "EVER" in margin of yellow card stock at bottom of layout. Layer one smaller paper daisy on top of larger one; poke brad through centers and attach to layout ⅞ inch from left side and overlapping seam between printed papers. Adhere arrow tab to layout 2⅝ inches from right edge and with top edges even. Thread floss through button; knot on front and adhere button to arrow tab. Tuck end of "delight" tag under button and adhere as shown.

Use computer to generate, or hand-print, journaling on white card stock to fit under hinged photo; adhere journaling to layout. Embellish underside of hinged photo with printed paper, catalog information, and remaining smaller daisy with brad affixed in center. Adhere additional catalog product information to main layout as desired. ■

SOURCES: Printed paper from K&Company; arrow tab from Creative Imaginations; tag, velvety stickers, paper daisies and brads from Making Memories; rub-on transfers from Heidi Grace Designs Inc. and Heidi Swapp; hinge from Daisy D's Paper Co.; permanent adhesive from Beacon; computer font from Two Peas In a Bucket Inc.

The day the UPS man pulled up to my house and started unloading two huge boxes, I was convinced he had the wrong address, until I saw my name clearly printed on the box labels. I was still completely perplexed as to what could be inside and who sent them. When I opened them and discovered the gorgeous dishes inside, I knew the surprise was compliments of my friend Dana Mees. We had been e-mailing and I mentioned I had seen some really pretty dishes in a mail order catalog. I was still going thru a divorce at the time and couldnt afford to buy them. I had no idea she would act on that e-mail. It still brings tears to my eyes when I think about it and I feel so lucky to have a friend who would be so kind and generous. It was the best kind of surprise ~ unexpected!

Materials

Color catalog images or photos: 5⅛ x 5¼-inch, 10 x 8-inch

Information/product descriptions cut from catalog

Card stock: yellow, white

Floral printed paper: blue, light green/pink

2¼ x 1¾-inch light green card-stock arrow tab

Tiny white card-stock "delight" tag

Black alphabet rub-on transfers: ¾-inch, 1¼-inch

1½-inch pink velvety alphabet stickers

2-inch light green hinge with 4 matching mini brads

Pink flat button

Pink paper daisies: 1½-inch, 2 (1⅛-inch)

2 deep pink brads

Yellow floss

Paper adhesive

Permanent adhesive

Computer with 2Peas Rickety font

Color printer

ATIJA

DESIGN BY EMILY DEISROTH

Inspiring thoughts are captured in the journaling of a life-changing trip recounted in this layout.

Project note: Adhere all elements using paper adhesive unless instructed otherwise.

Print selected accent photo onto shrink film; punch holes in upper corners. Shrink film following manufacturer's instructions.

Tear 12-inch strips of varying widths from floral and windowpanes printed papers; adhere to 12-inch square of gold metallic card stock as desired, overlapping some strips. Tear a 4½ x 6-inch corner from a piece of tan card stock; adhere to upper left corner of layout.

Print three photos; adhere to layout as shown, leaving lower right quadrant open. *Note: On sample, photos measure 6 x 4 and 4 x 6 inches.*

Book: Use computer to generate journaling on a document measuring 3½ x 9¼ inches; print on speckled beige paper and trim to size. Adhere journaling to reverse side of handmade paper; trim or tear edges of handmade paper even with journaling. With journaling face up, fold top down and bottom up to meet in the center. Turn journaling facedown; center and adhere a 24-inch strand of twine down book cover using an adhesive dot. Turn journaling face up; fold up bottom panel and bottom portion of twine. Set mini brads in holes in shrink-film photo; adhere photo over twine to bottom panel of book.

Use computer to generate title or journaling for book cover on a document measuring 3⅜ x 1⅛ inches; print on speckled beige paper and trim to size. Fold down top panel of book and top portion of twine; adhere title to top panel over twine. Tie beads to ends of twine; tie twine ends to close book. Adhere book to lower right corner of layout using craft glue. Adhere charms to layout using craft glue. ■

SOURCES: Shrink film from Ink-Jet; mini brads from Making Memories; adhesive applicator from Xyron.

Materials

Digital photos	Photo paper	Copper mini brads	Computer with photo-editing
Card stock: gold metallic, tan	Printable shrink film	Hole punch	software
Printed paper: cream/gold floral,	Teal handmade paper	Adhesive applicator	Printer
gold/beige windowpanes,	Fine natural twine	Paper adhesive	
speckled beige	Complementary beads, charms	Craft glue	

Knowing Atija has given me strength at my weakest moments. When I am poor, I feel wealthy; and when I am tired, I know that I can accomplish more. Thank you Atija.

SAND
DESIGN BY TAMI MAYBERRY

Subtle, coordinating papers and a simple photo are the perfect background for reflective journaling.

Project note: *Adhere all elements using paper adhesive unless instructed otherwise.*

Adhere a 3¼ x 12-inch strip of paisley paper vertically near the left edge of a 12-inch square of horizontal stripe paper. Use computer to generate journaling to fit within an area measuring 10 x 5⅜ inches; print out onto burgundy paper. Trim, centering journaling near bottom edge of an 11x 8-inch rectangle. Adhere journaling panel to layout as shown.

Cut 8½ x 1-inch strips from paisley and floral papers. Adhere paisley strip across top edge of journaling with right edges even; adhere floral strip overlapping paisley strip as shown. Adhere a ½ x 8-inch strip of floral paper over bottom edge of journaling panel as shown, aligning right edge even with right edge of layout.

Adhere die-cut letters to spell "sand" along bottom edge of a 5 x 2½-inch piece of burgundy paper, positioning word toward right edge. Apply alphabet rub-on transfers to spell "A" and "look at the" above "sand" as shown, leaving room to attach the metal "simple" tag with craft glue. Referring to photo, adhere title panel to upper right corner of layout.

Adhere one 4½ x ½-inch strip of paisley paper to layout just below title panel; make "n" in "sand" overlap top edge of strip. Adhere a second 4½ x ½-inch strip of paisley paper down left edge of journaling panel as shown.

Adhere photo at an angle across upper left corner of layout; attach photo turns over left edge of photo with mini brads. Apply alphabet rub-on transfers to spell "sand" on lower left corner of photo. ■

SOURCES: Printed paper from Chatterbox; die-cut letters from Ellison/Sizzix; rub-on transfers from Royal & Langnickel; metal tag from All My Memories; photo turns and mini brads from Junkitz.

Materials

7 x 5-inch photo

Printed papers: burgundy/pink/ brown: stripe, floral, paisley; solid burgundy

1½-inch tan die-cut letters to spell "sand"

Alphabet rub-on transfers

1-inch oval metal "simple" tag

2 white photo turns

2 white mini brads

Paper adhesive

Craft glue

AFTER THE FLOOD

DESIGN BY STEPHANIE BARNARD

Have an unusually long story to tell? Try stacking the photos above long blocks of text.

Project note: Adhere elements using double-sided tape unless instructed otherwise.

Photos: Cut a strip of card stock the width of your photos and long enough to accommodate a photo on each panel when strip is folded accordion-style. Score and fold strip; adhere a photo to each panel, leaving last panel open for adhering to layout. Repeat three more times for the double-page, four-column layout shown in photo.

Journaling: Use computer to generate, or hand-print, journaling onto solid-color card stock to fit within an area approximately 5¾ x 6¼ inches. Trim journaling panel to 5¾ x 10¼ inches with journaling at bottom. Repeat three more times using different solid colors of card stock for the layout shown in photo.

Layout: Die-cut letters for each column title from card stock; adhere letters to 4 x 1-inch strips cut from contrasting solid-color card stock. Adhere journaling panels and titles to 12-inch-square sheets of printed card stock side by side as shown. Adhere last panel of photo accordions to top unprinted areas of journaling panels using adhesive dots. Add details with fine-tip marker as desired. ■

SOURCES: Printed card stock from American Crafts; die-cutting machine and dies from Ellison/Sizzix; tape and adhesive dots from Therm O Web.

Materials

Photos	Solid-color card stock: blue, dark	Die-cutting machine with	Adhesive dots
Brown/orange/green/blue	blue, green, orange	⅝-inch alphabet dies	Computer with font of
striped printed card stock	Black fine-tip marker	Double-sided tape	your choice
			Printer

WINTER FROST

DESIGN BY SHERRY WRIGHT

Brightly colored pictures and papers warm up winter memories in this layout and bonus photo folder.

Layout: Adhere circles printed paper to cover card stock, positioning a circle in the upper right corner as shown. Adhere a 12 x 4½-inch piece of striped paper across bottom of layout, bottom and side edges even, with stripes running horizontally. Adhere a 2 x 5½-inch piece of green snowflakes paper down right side of layout 2½ inches from top edge.

Adhere 5 x 7-inch photo at an angle in upper left corner of layout; adhere "Winter" transparency over photo. Wrap hot pink ribbon around upper left corner of layout; adhere ends on reverse side. Adhere metal snowflake plaque over ribbon as shown. Adhere a 2-inch piece of gingham-checked ribbon over lower left corner of photo; center and adhere snowflake spangle to ribbon.

CONTNUED ON PAGE 166

Materials

Color photos: 5 x 7-inch, 6 x 4-inch, 8 smaller photos

12-inch square card stock

Printed paper: pink/blue/ orange/green: circles, stripes; orange-on-orange plaid, green-on-green snowflakes

Pink/blue/orange/green circles/ plaid reversible 6 x 4½-inch file folder with complementary- color file pages

"Winter" printed transparency

Winter definitions card-stock alphabet stencils

Winter-themed card-stock stickers

3 bottle caps

3 (1-inch) snowflake bottle cap stickers: red, green

Rub-on transfers: 1½-inch blue "Winter," 2-inch white "Frost," assorted winter-themed

Embossing ink pad

Silver embossing powder

Fine-tip black marker

Ribbons: ⅝-inch-wide hot pink with black stitching, ¼-inch-wide black-and-white gingham-checked

Black-and-white ribbon photo corners

Small flat buttons: pink, aqua

White snowflake spangles

Tiny magenta crystals

1½ x 2-inch metal snowflake plaque

⅝-inch metal snowflake brad

Mailbox-style "W" tile

Multicolored paper clips

Red medium binder clip

Rubber mallet

Die-cutting machine with converter for flattening bottle caps (optional)

Stapler with silver staples

Heat-embossing tool

Jewel-setting tool

Fine sandpaper

Adhesive-backed hook-and- loop fastening tape

Paper adhesive

BIRTHDAY GIRL

DESIGN BY MELISSA SMITH

A pink, frilly "gift bag" opens to provide additional space for photos on this birthday celebration scrapbook page.

Project notes: Ink edges of all photos, card stock, printed paper and die cuts before adhering them to the layout. Adhere elements using paper adhesive unless instructed otherwise.

Center and adhere an 11¾-inch square of pink card stock to a 12-inch square of pink paisley paper; center and adhere an 11-inch square of light green paisley paper to pink card stock.

"Birthday Girl" corner frame and gift-bag tag: Working within word-processing program, open "Insert" menu; choose "Textbox." Choose font; set size at 59 points and type "Birthday Girl." From pop-up dialogue box, select "Change Text Direction" for "Birthday" textbox. In the same manner, set "happy birthday" in 18-point type around sides and bottom of an area measuring 1½ x 2¼ inches for gift-bag tag; set age numeral in 45-point type in center. Print frame and gift tag onto white card stock; trim.

Journaling: Use computer to generate, or hand-print, journaling to run under main photo on an 8 x 2⅝-inch strip of white card stock, positioning text toward left end to fit around die cut in lower left corner. *Note: On sample, text area measures 4 x 1⅝ inches.*

Use computer to generate, or hand-print, additional journaling—names of party guests, party activities, etc.—onto printable transparency to fit on right side of layout. *Note: On sample, text area measures 3½ x 2⅜ inches.*

Gift-bag mini book: Stack two 6¾ x 3¾-inch pieces of white card stock, edges even; fold in half to create a 3⅜ x 3¾-inch book. Staple along fold. Center and adhere a 3½ x 3¾-inch piece of pink striped paper to front of book.

Adhere smaller photos to inside pages, embellishing pages as desired with printed paper and ribbon; use computer to generate, or hand-print, journaling on strips of white card stock to fit on pages. Adhere "happy birthday" tag to front; adhere pink ribbon bow at top of tag. Hot-glue ends of gift-bag handle to reverse side of front cover; hot-glue marabou feathers across top edge of cover.

Layout: Adhere "Birthday Girl" frame to layout 1½ inches from top edge of layout and 1 inch from left edge; adhere pink ribbon bow in corner and rhinestone at each end. Arrange 5⅜ x 6¼-inch main photo, larger flower die-cut, card-stock journaling panel and printed transparency on layout as shown, with photo overlapping journaling panel and transparency, and die-cut overlapping journaling and lower left corner of photo and overhanging corner of layout. Adhere elements to layout; adhere three rhinestones down right edge of journaling.

Adhere smaller die cut in upper right corner of layout. Cut out three white card-stock photo corners; adhere to 4¾ x 3-inch photo. Adhere photo to pink card stock; trim, leaving narrow borders. Adhere photo to upper right corner of layout, overlapping die cut. Adhere gift-bag mini book in lower right corner. ∎

SOURCES: Printed paper, die cuts and ribbon from Anna Griffin Inc.; marabou feathers from Midwest Design Imports; computer font and Word word-processing software from Microsoft.

Materials

Color photos: 5⅜ x 6½-inch,
   4¾ x 3-inch, 6–8 smaller
   photos ranging in size from
   1½ inches square to 2½ x
   3⅝ inches

Card stock: pink, white

Printed paper: white/pink
   paisley, white/light green

paisley, pink/white stripe,
   pink-on-pink, pink/green
   stripe

Printable transparency

Black ink pad

Flower die cuts: 5 x 3-inch, 3½ x
   2¼-inch

5½-inch strip of handle cut from
   gift bag

Fine-tip black marker (optional)

5 crystal rhinestones

⅜-inch-wide ribbon: pink satin,
   pink/green/blue stripe

Light pink marabou feathers

Stapler with staples

Paper adhesive

Hot-glue gun

Computer with Copperplate
   Gothic Light font and word-
   processing program

Printer

GIRLIE SECRETS

DESIGN BY MELISSA SMITH

Whimsical doodling and playful pixies add a touch of Victorian charm to this layout.

Project note: Ink edges of all photos and card-stock pieces before adhering them. Adhere elements using paper adhesive unless instructed otherwise.

Working within scrapbooking software, use digital stamping brushes to position dotted circles, diamonds and journaling box on an 8½ x 11-inch layout as shown. *Note: On sample, dotted circles measure (from top down) 4½ inches, 2¾ inches and 3½ inches in diameter. Block of diamonds measures 4 x 2½ inches. Journaling box measures 4⅜ x 3 inches.* Add digital swirls, fairies and flower borders to layout as desired. Type journaling inside journaling box. Print page onto an 8½ x 11-inch sheet of white card stock.

Bring up circle shape within scrapbooking software; size a circle to fit within each dotted circle. Change color to "transparent" and place photos within circles. Print photos; trim and adhere inside dotted circles, allowing edge of bottom photo to extend beyond edge of layout.

Trim one end of a 7-inch piece of pink ribbon at an angle; adhere down upper left side of layout near edge. Adhere a 5-inch piece of pink ribbon across lower right corner near bottom edge, allowing 1¼ inches to extend beyond right edge; fringe protruding end with scissors.

Print title onto white card stock within an area measuring 4 x 1⅝ inches; trim to size. Adhere title to light yellow-green card stock and cut out using decorative-edge scissors. Using adhesive dots, adhere title over upper left corner of layout so edges protrude ½ inch beyond top and left edges of page. Adhere ⅛-inch rhinestone to paper flower; adhere to upper right corner of title panel as shown.

Using decorative-edge scissors, cut a 2¼ x 2¼-inch photo corner from light yellow-green card stock; stamp with swirl rubber stamp. Adhere to lower right corner of layout using adhesive dots, allowing photo corner to extend ¼ inch beyond bottom and right edges.

Punch or cut three hearts in various sizes from pink, glossy gold and glossy black card stock; arrange over ribbon between journaling and bottom photo as shown. Adhere hearts to layout using adhesive dots for gold and black hearts. Adhere a paper flower with ⁵⁄₁₆-inch rhinestone center to hearts. Arrange flowers in clusters between photos and over central swirl; add rhinestone centers as desired. Adhere flowers to layout, adhering some with adhesive dots for added dimension.

Tint journaling square just inside border using chalk. Adhere ⁵⁄₁₆-inch pink rhinestones to corners.

Thread silver charm onto green ribbon; tie in a bow and adhere to pink ribbon on left side of layout. ∎

SOURCES: SL Woodcut Faeries Font by Su Lucas; stamping brushes from www.ScrapArtist.com; swirl stamp kit from www.TwoPeasinaBucket.com; rubber stamps from Autumn Leaves; chalk from Koss; rhinestones from The Beadery; flowers from Prima, Doodlebug Design Inc. and Ampad; scrapbooking software from Hewlett Packard.

girlie
Secrets

Remember playing like you were fairies in the forest in the yard, especially when all the Azaleas were in bloom? Such pretty girls ... such a pretty time.

Materials

3 digital photos

Digital elements: woodcut fairies, distressed stamping brushes, swirl stamp

Card stock: white, light yellow-green, glossy gold, glossy black

Photo paper

Swirl rubber stamps

Black ink pad

Black fine-tip pen

Light green chalk

Silver charm

Rhinestones: 5/16-inch pink, gold;

1/8-inch pink, light green

3/8- to 1-inch paper flowers: pink, yellow, gold, lavender

Ribbons: 5/16-inch-wide green, 1/2-inch-wide pink

3/4- to 1 3/8-inch heart punches (optional)

Decorative-edge scissors

Paper adhesive

Adhesive dots

Computer with fonts of your choice and scrapbooking software

Printer

SEA

DESIGN BY SHERRY WRIGHT

Journaling on a clear overlay becomes an unobtrusive but integral part of this serene layout.

Project notes: *Adhere photo, paper and transparency using paper adhesive. Adhere remaining elements using craft glue.*

Adhere printed paper to 12 x 12-inch card stock to cover, with paper's stripes running horizontally. Center and adhere photo to top of layout ⅛ inch from top edge.

Arrange fabric strips in overlapping waves across bottom of layout; using a variety of stitches, machine-stitch over fabric waves, allowing strips to fold and fray for a random, natural look. Staple over ends of strips. Trim ends, leaving a little excess fabric.

Paint bookplate light blue; sand lightly. Tie short lengths of fabric strip through holes in ends. Feed a ¼-inch-wide strip of light blue card stock through label maker; imprint with sentiment. Using distress ink, ink strip lightly to make words stand out. Adhere strip to layout near bottom of layout 3¼ inches from right edge. Adhere bookplate over strip to frame sentiment.

Sand edges of coasters; apply circle rub-on transfer to diamonds coaster and adhere coaster at an angle to upper left corner of layout, overlapping photo.

Adhere alphabet stickers over remaining coasters to spell "SEA" with "E" on circle-print coaster. Arrange coasters in upper right corner of layout as shown, overlapping edges and positioning them at angles.

Use computer to generate, or hand-print, journaling onto transparency to fit within an open area of photo (on sample project, approximately 4½ x 2¾ inches); trim and adhere transparency over photo. ∎

SOURCES: Printed paper, chipboard coasters, alphabet stickers and fabric strips from Imagination Project/Gin-X; distress ink from Ranger Industries Inc.; bookplate from Making Memories; label maker and tape from DYMO Corp.; adhesive from Beacon.

Materials

10½ x 8½-inch color photo	Distress ink	Stapler with staples	Craft glue
Lime card stock	Light blue craft paint	Label maker	Computer with font of
Blue/lime striped printed paper	Circle rub-on transfer	Fine sandpaper	your choice
Printable transparency	Assorted blue 1⅞- to 3-inch	Paintbrush	Printer
4 (2-inch-square) blue/lime	alphabet stickers to spell "SEA"	Sewing machine with light	
chipboard coasters	Blue/green/white fabric strips	blue-gray thread	
Fine-tip black marker (optional)	3 x ¾-inch bookplate	Paper adhesive	

SEA

This Fall you were finally able to "sea" your first glimpse of Lake Huron via boat. Since you've always had a love of boats I thought the ferry to Mackinac Island would be a good first boat trip. We met Grandma & Grandpa in St. Ignace and off we... Who knew a toddler could be so quiet... you didn't speak a word just stared in amazement at the water, Mackinac bridge, and lighthouse that we passed by. What a fun day with a horse drawn carriage ride and a trip to the butterfly house. Just think You were one tired but happy boy on the trip home. Oct. 2005

BOYS OF SUMMER

DESIGN BY EMILY DEISROTH

A summer's worth of memories are displayed in photos and recalled in the journaling on this simple scrapbook page.

Using photo-editing software, alter photos, converting some to black-and-white and manipulating color as desired. Size main photo at 5¼ x 3¾ inches; size two identical photos at 1¾ x 2¾ inches for sides; size remaining photos so that you can create a continuous strip of photos 1 inch high across 12-inch layout. **Note:** *On sample layout, the smaller photos for the continuous strip fade from color to black-and-white as they progress across the page, showing the passage of time.* Print photos and trim.

Journaling: Working within photo-editing program, crop digital photo of sand so that only sand is visible. Set transparency level at 70 percent. Create a new 11-inch-square document; place photo of sand onto new document, stretching it to fill bottom third of document. Type journaling over sand; print onto 11-inch square of white card stock.

Print sand onto a smaller piece of white card stock; trim one edge in an irregular line and adhere to upper right corner of white card stock with journaling.

Side tags: Working within photo-editing program, create two documents measuring 1¾ x 2¾ inches. Type desired sentiments onto documents; "flip" documents to reverse type. Print out onto transparency; trim each size.

Title: Working within photo-editing program, create a document measuring 11 x 8½ inches. Type a title; click "flip" to reverse type; print out onto transparency.

Layout: Center and adhere white card stock with journaling to 12-inch square of gray card stock. Adhere title transparency to top of white card stock, edges even, applying adhesive where it will be concealed by photos. Adhere smaller photos in a continuous strip across page above journaling. Center and adhere main photo and side photos to layout below title as shown.

Using matches or hand-held candlelighter, melt edges of small transparencies to give them texture and depth. To melt a hole in transparency, hold flame 3 inches below transparency at the spot where you want the hole; when hole begins to form, immediately remove flame. For each small transparency, knot a 3-inch piece of ribbon around a safety pin; trim ends. Adhere one at top edge of each transparency; adhere transparencies over side photos. ■

SOURCES: Transparencies from 3M; ribbon from Making Memories.

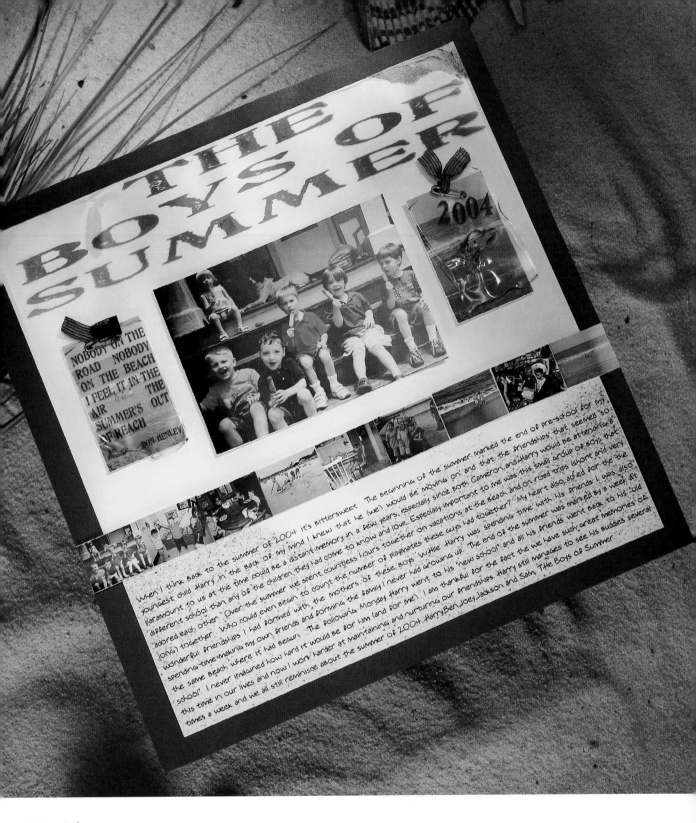

Materials

Digital photos: sand or other
background texture, plus
10–12 photos as desired

Card stock: white, gray

Glossy photo paper

Printable transparencies

2 (1-inch) antique-tone safety
pins

⅜-inch-wide gold/gray ribbon

Matches or candlelighter

Paper adhesive

Computer with fonts of
your choice and photo-
editing software

Wide-format printer

When I was about 10 years old, Gary and I went out on the jetty. We laughed and talked the whole way out, not realizing the tide was coming in. As the waves crashed closer to us, we decided to turn back. Several of the rocks had been devoured by the ocean. At one particular spot, Gary determined that the only way to cross was to jump. He went first. Just as he landed, his foot hit the dreaded green slime and he slipped in. When he stood up, he was covered head to toe with slime. I still laugh when I remember seeing him at that moment!

Journaling 04/2006

green slime

GREEN SLIME

DESIGN BY RACHAEL GIALLONGO

Eeeuuuwww! Chipboard elements and a block of handprinted journaling bring to mind past adventures.

Project note: Adhere photo and paper using paper adhesive. Adhere remaining elements using craft glue.

Paint chipboard brackets cream.

Tear one short edge off a 6⅜ x 11-inch piece of turquoise card stock; adhere to right side of an 11½-inch square of beige card stock ⅛ inch from right edge with top edges even. Tear one long edge off an 11½ x 2-inch strip of printed paper; adhere across top of beige card stock with top and side edges even. Center and adhere photo to turquoise card stock just below torn printed paper edge. Using both the chipboard stencil outlines and the punched-out letters, arrange lettering for title on turquoise card stock below photo; adhere. Attach mini brads in a row near bottom right corner of turquoise card stock.

Center and adhere beige card-stock square with photo panel to 12-inch-square of pale turquoise card stock. Adhere ribbon across top of layout ¾ inch from top edge; wrap ends over edge to reverse side and adhere.

Add journaling to left side of beige card stock using fine-tip marker. Adhere brackets to card stock as shown, framing journaling at top and bottom. ■

SOURCES: Printed paper from My Mind's Eye; chipboard brackets from Heidi Swapp; chipboard stencils from Scenic Route Paper Co.; ribbon from Offray.

Materials

4 x 6-inch color photo	Chipboard embellishments: 2	Black fine-tip marker	Paintbrush
Card stock: pale turquoise,	(3-inch-wide) brackets, black	3 pale green mini brads	Paper adhesive
turquoise, beige	1½ x 2-inch alphabet stencils	¹¹⁄₁₆-inch-wide white-and-beige	Craft glue
Green/brown/blue striped	Cream craft paint	pin-dot grosgrain ribbon	
printed paper			

Materials

8 x 10-inch color photo

12-inch-square of card stock, any color

Printed paper: leaf print, green/blue swirl, green/white diamonds, blue/green "SEASONS"

Tea-dyed printable self-adhesive cotton sheet

Metal leaf plaque

Fabric: 2 (20-inch) squares for pillow front and back, assorted scraps in complementary colors for leaves

20-inch square heavyweight interfacing

18-inch-square pillow form

Embossing pens

Black fine-tip marker

Hand-sewing needle

Sewing machine with coordinating threads

Iron

Paper adhesive

½ yard fusible heavy-duty adhesive

Scanner

Computer with photo-editing software and stitching program

Printer

SEASONS

DESIGN BY SHERRY WRIGHT AND RUTHANN WILLIS

Create a stylish accent pillow with a layout image nestled among appliquéd leaves.

Paper layout: Adhere a 12-inch square of blue/green swirl paper to card stock. Adhere a 3 x 12-inch strip of diamonds printed paper to right side of layout, ½ inch from right edge. Adhere photo to layout toward right side, overlapping diamonds paper.

Trim leaf outlines along right side of a 12-inch square of leaves printed paper so that leaves will "frame" and enhance photo when adhered over left side of layout. Adhere trimmed leaves paper to layout, overlapping photo, with top, left and bottom edges even.

Using a blue embossing pen, highlight the metal leaf plaque; adhere plaque to lower right corner of photo. Trim "SEASONS" from printed paper; adhere to layout along lower left corner of photo as shown. Add journaling along border of photo as desired using a fine-tip marker or pen.

Scanning and printing onto cotton sheet: When ink and glue on paper layout have dried, place half of layout facedown on scanner. Select "Preview" and adjust borders to scan entire half of page; scan and save image on computer. Repeat to scan and save second half of image.

Open both halves within stitching program on computer. Merge images and adjust borders as desired. Preview merged image and save on computer.

Working in photo-editing program, resize image to measure 8 inches square. Choose "Print," then "Printing Preferences"; change setting to "Best Photo" and choose "Premium Photo Paper" option. Load cotton sheet into printer and print image onto cotton sheet.

Pillow: Apply fusible adhesive to backs of coordinating fabrics to be used for leaves. Using patterns provided (page 171), cut 28–30 leaf images from assorted adhesive-backed fabrics.

Fold one 20-inch fabric square in half for front; press with iron to crease lightly. Fold fabric in half in opposite direction and repeat. Intersection of creases is center of pillow front.

Cut around 8-inch printed image on cotton sheet leaving ¼-inch borders. Peel backing from image; center and adhere image to pillow front. Pin a 20-inch square of interfacing to reverse side of pillow front at corners with edges even.

Adjust sewing machine to sew a 2.5-width zigzag stitch; set stitch length for a close satin stitch. Machine-stitch a sample onto scrap fabric; refine adjustments and machine-stitch over edges of photo image. Arrange adhesive-backed leaves around photo; machine-stitch around edges of leaves using a variety of satin and fancy stitches.

Pin pillow front and back together, right sides facing and edges even. Machine-stitch around edges using a straight stitch and leaving a 10-inch opening in the center of one side for turning. Clip corners; turn pillow right side out. Insert pillow form through opening. Turn under fabric edges along opening; hand-stitch to close opening using invisible slip stitches. ∎

SOURCES: Printed papers from Cherry Arte; self-adhesive cotton sheet from DMD; metal plaque from Pressed Petals; embossing pens from Sakura; HeatnBond fusible adhesive; Photoshop Elements 2.0 from Adobe Systems Inc.; PhotoStitch from Canon.

PATTERNS ON PAGE 171

Materials

- 3⅛ x 4-inch black-and-white photo
- 2 (5 x 5 x 1½-inch) stretched canvases
- Green/blue striped printed paper
- Die cuts: 3 (2½ x 1¼-inch) tags, 1½-inch blue heart frame, 3

- (¾-inch) photo corners, 1 slide mount
- Alphabet stamps
- Black ink
- Paint: blue, light blue, white
- 1¼-inch wooden letters for initials
- 3 white flower brads

- Blue brad
- Silver alphabet slide charms to spell "LOVE"
- Silver flower charm on ball chain
- Small white paper clip
- White jumbo rickrack
- 1½-inch white silk flower

- ½-inch heart punch
- Paintbrushes
- Foam brushes
- Stapler with blue staples
- Decoupage medium
- Adhesive dots
- Double-sided tape

"KJ" CANVAS

DESIGN BY STEPHANIE BARNARD

This coordinating set of artfully decorated stretched canvases will add charm to any room decor.

Project note: *Use double-sided tape to adhere elements unless instructed otherwise.*

Paint canvases blue with foam brush; add lighter blue and white highlights along sides. Sand sides of canvases. Using decoupage medium, adhere 5-inch squares of printed paper to cover fronts of canvases.

Photo canvas: Adhere photo to canvas front as shown; adhere die-cut photo corners to top corners and bottom left corner of photo. Brush decoupage medium over canvas including photo. Adhere rickrack across canvas ½ inch from bottom edge, extending ends over sides to back; in the same fashion, adhere rickrack around the upper right corner of canvas. Adhere silk flower to upper right corner of canvas.

Paint die-cut slide mount blue; let dry. Stamp "beauty" onto printed paper; trim to fit in window of slide mount and adhere to reverse side. Attach flower brad to a ¼-inch-wide strip of printed paper; adhere across slide mount and trim ends even. Wrap another strip of printed paper around upper right corner of slide mount; adhere ends on reverse side. Slide paper clip over top edge of slide mount. Adhere slide mount at an angle to lower right corner of canvas using adhesive dots.

"KJ" canvas: Brush decoupage medium over canvas. Adhere rickrack across lower edge in the same fashion as for first canvas; adhere rickrack around the upper left corner. Adhere random pieces torn from printed paper to die-cut tags; trim edges even with edges of tags. Stamp one tag each with "happy" and "DREAM." From blue portions of printed paper, die-cut ½-inch heart and cut ¼-inch-wide strip to fit on tag; adhere heart over strip on "DREAM" tag. On top tag, thread "LOVE" slide charms onto a ¼-inch-wide strip cut from printed paper; staple ends of strip to tag. Attach flower brad to corner of "LOVE" tag. Thread blue brad through holes of all three tags; fan out tags and adhere to canvas using adhesive dots.

String die-cut heart frame onto ball chain of flower charm; adhere charm to upper right corner of canvas using an adhesive dot; adhere die-cut heart to center area of canvas ⅜ inch from right edge.

Cut pieces from printed paper to cover fronts of wooden initials; adhere using decoupage medium. Paint sides and edges of initials blue, allowing some paint to show around edges of front surface. Sand edges; adhere initials to lower left corner of canvas. Adhere flower brad to first initial. ■

SOURCES: Stretched canvases from Fredrix Artist Canvas; printed paper from Daisy D's Paper Co.; die cuts from Ellison/Sizzix; stamps and ink from Plaid Enterprises/All Night Media; paints, wooden letters and decoupage medium from Plaid Enterprises; flower brads from Creative Impressions; alphabet charms from PM Designs; flower charm from Dolphin Enterprises; adhesive dots and double-sided tape from Therm O Web.

THE GREAT OUTDOORS

DESIGN BY LORINE MASON

Stitched and layered fleece creates dimensional waves of water on this layout design.

Project note: Use a straight stitch and light blue thread for all machine stitching.

Lay photo on top of light blue fleece; trim fleece close to edges using pinking shears. Lay photo and fleece on 12-inch square of printed paper as shown. Machine-stitch around edges of photo through all layers.

Using pinking shears, cut waves along one long edge of a 13 x 2½-inch strip of blue fleece, a 13 x 2½-inch strip of light blue fleece, and a 13 x 5½-inch piece of blue fleece. Lay narrower blue strip across layout, overlapping bottom edge of photo; machine-stitch through all layers along edges of waves. Lay light blue fleece strip across layout, overlapping bottom of first strip; machine-stitch through all layers along edges of waves. Lay wider blue strip on layout, overlapping bottom of light blue strip and covering bottom of layout; machine-stitch through all layers along edges of waves.

Fold up third strip of fleece; trim away underlying fleece from first and second strips. Fold blue fleece down; machine-stitch several overlapping waves across it.

Lay vellum quotation and title on top of light blue fleece; trim close to edges using pinking shears. Lay quotation and fleece on layout in upper right corner; machine-stitch around edges. Center vellum title and fleece on layout 1 inch from bottom edge; machine-stitch around edges.

Machine-stitch around edges of layout ¼ inch from edges of paper; using straight scissors, trim fleece even with edges of paper. ■

SOURCE: Printed paper from Paper House Productions.

Materials

4 x 6-inch color photo	Vellum quotation and title	Pinking shears	Sewing machine and light blue thread
Seascape printed paper	Fleece: blue, light blue		

Find *what* brings you *joy* and go there.

the *Great* Outdoors

Children, children,
don't forget
There are elves
and fairies yet
Where the knotty
hawthorne grows.

Look for prints
of fairy toes.
Where the grassy
rings are green.
Moonlight dances
will be seen

SWEET

HAPP

precious

believe

cherish

in
faiRies

BELIEVE IN FAIRIES

DESIGN BY KRISTEN SWAIN

All the sweetness of little girls and fairies is captured on this charming embellished clipboard.

Project note: Use decoupage medium as adhesive throughout.

Paint clipboard, including metal clip, with white; when dry, sand edges. Adhere striped paper to bottom 3 inches of clipboard; trim edges even. Adhere floral paper to cover remaining section of clipboard, trimming top to fit paper around metal clip.

Adhere photos, fairy and flower cutouts, and decorative brad to clipboard. Use computer to generate fairy poem onto manila tags. Thread fibers through holes in tags, attaching a charm to fibers in bottom tag. Adhere tags to right side of clipboard near top, tucking ends under photo as shown. Adhere flower cutout to metal clip. Thread assorted ribbons and lace through hole in metal clip; knot. Tie charm to metal clip using a length of fiber.

Adhere polka-dot ribbon and 1¼-inch-wide sheer ribbon over seam between printed papers. Use computer to generate outlines of individual letters for "believe" onto pink card stock; cut out letters using craft knife and adhere to bottom of clipboard toward right edge, overlapping ribbon slightly. Adhere black alphabet stickers to spell "in fairies" below "believe" in lower right corner of clipboard. Embellish clipboard with additional rub-on transfers and epoxy stickers as desired. Adhere silk daisy 1 inch from left edge over ribbon. Apply epoxy flower stickers to dominoes; adhere to clipboard in lower left corner. ■

SOURCES: Printed paper from K&Company; fairy and flower cutouts from Wallies; epoxy stickers from Creative Imaginations; rub-on transfers and brad from Making Memories; stickers from Better Homes & Gardens and me & my BIG ideas; charms from Craft Supply; ribbons and fibers from Li'l Davis Designs and Craft Supply; decoupage medium from Plaid Enterprises; computer font from Two Peas in a Bucket Inc.

Materials

Sepia-tone photos	Epoxy stickers: words, flowers	Large decorative brad	Fuzzy fibers: white, pale blue
Clipboard	Black alphabet stickers	2 gold fairy charms	White silk daisy
Pink card stock	Black alphabet rub-on transfers	Ribbons: ½-inch-wide cream/	Fine sandpaper
Light blue wallpaper-print	Flower rub-on transfers or	pin-dot, ¼-inch- and	Craft knife
printed papers: stripe, floral	transparent stickers	1¼-inch-wide sheer white	Small foam brushes
2 (4 x 2-inch) manila tags	White paint	organza, ⅜-inch-wide cream	Decoupage medium
Wallpaper cutouts:	2 (1¼ x ⅝-inch) light-colored	lace trim, ¼-inch- and ⅜-inch-	Fiddlesticks font
fairies, flowers	dominoes	wide pink satin	Computer and printer

PHOTO CALENDAR PAGES

DESIGN BY EMILY DEISROTH

Mini photos from everyday and extra-special events fill the pages of this special memories calendar.

Using photo-editing software, print photos in contact sheet format. Trim photos to size, making some smaller than others. **Note:** *On sample, photos measure 1 to 1¼ inches square.* Print calendar grid onto card stock or printed paper, or use pages from an actual calendar. Punch 2-inch squares from desired colors of card stock or printed paper for matting or edging photos; ink edges as desired. **Option:** *Cut card stock squares or shapes to size.* Adhere photos to card-stock and printed-paper squares; adhere photos to calendar page.

Embellish individual photos and blank calendar squares as desired, choosing embellishments that accentuate the season and events. The sample shown includes printed woven labels, chipboard arrow and circle accents, photo turns attached with mini brads, rub-on transfers, card-stock stickers, and acrylic embellishments. Add journaling using pens of different colors. ■

SOURCES: Printed paper from American Crafts and KI Memories; card-stock stickers from 7gypsies, Magnetic Poetry and KI Memories; chipboard and acrylic embellishments from KI Memories; rub-on transfers from 7gypsies and Making Memories; woven labels from me & my BIG ideas and 7gypsies; square punch from Marvy.

Materials

Digital photos or color photos cropped to 1–1¼ inches square	Printed papers in desired patterns	Acrylic embellishments	2-inch square punch
	Card-stock stickers	Printed woven labels	Paper adhesive
Calendar pages (optional)	Chipboard embellishments: arrows, ⅜-inch dots	Photo turns	Computer with calendar and photo-editing programs
Card stock in desired colors	Rub-on transfers	Mini brads	Printer
		Brown ink pad	
		Colored fine-tip pens	

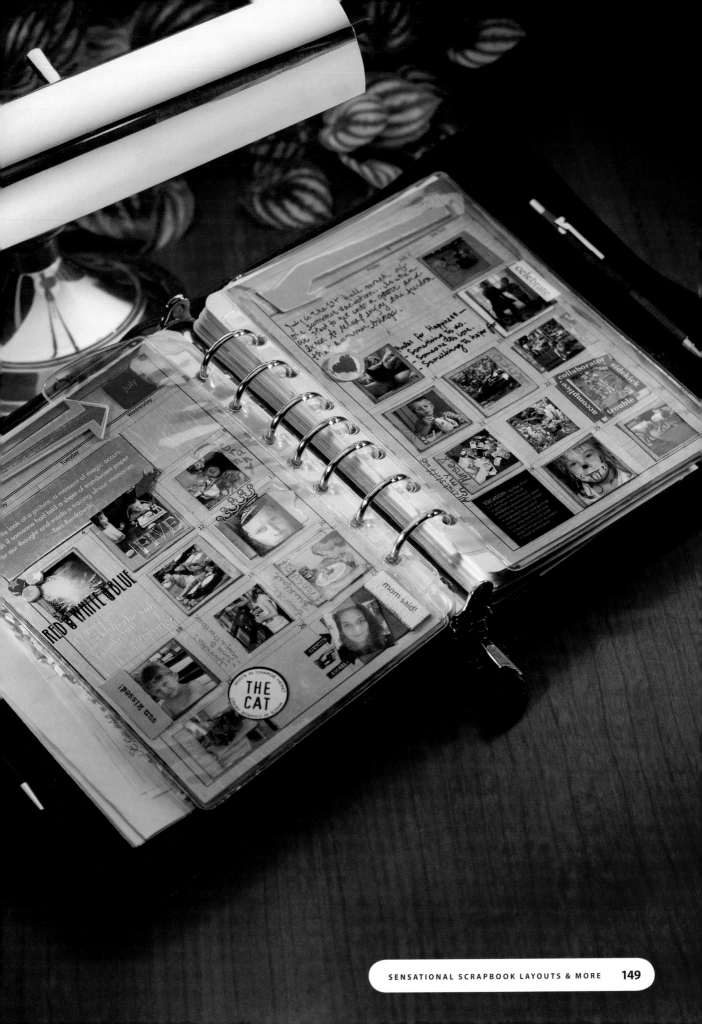

Innocent

Lovable

Sweet

FRAME OF ENDEARMENTS

DESIGN BY KATHLEEN PANEITZ

Sweet sentiments and an adorable pet picture are the focal points of this framed layout.

Cut gray card stock to fit inside frame. Adhere floral tape across card stock near top edge. Adhere photo to white card stock and trim, leaving narrow borders; adhere photo to upper left corner of layout. Adhere a 2-inch strip of striped tape vertically over upper left corner of layout, overlapping photo 1 inch from left edge.

Adhere sentiments cut from tape along right edge of photo; apply rub-on transfers to spell "Sweet," overlapping lower right corner of photo as shown. Adhere coasters across layout, referring to photo for placement. Insert layout in frame. ■

SOURCES: Frame from JoAnn's; cotton tape and coasters from Center City Designs/Imagination Project; rub-on transfers from Gin-X/Imagination Project; adhesive from Beacon.

Materials

5⅛ x 4-inch color photo	⅝-inch-wide pink/brown/	1⅞-inch pink/brown/blue	Craft adhesive
10¼-inch-square cream frame	blue printed cotton tape:	coasters: striped, 2 floral	
with ribbon hanger	striped, floral, brown/white	Brown alphabet rub-on	
Card stock: gray, white	sentiments	transfers: 2½-inch, ½-inch	

APPRECIATION BOUQUET

DESIGN BY MELISSA SMITH

Bright blossoms, sweet pictures and thoughtful cards fill this bouquet that is sure to delight any teacher!

Project note: Ink edges of photos, card stock and printed paper before adhering them.

On computer, type "I'm grateful for you because …" repeatedly so that when a sheet of card stock is printed, it can be cut into 2¾ x 2-inch rectangles with the phrase printed across the top of each. Print card stock in a variety of colors; cut apart and ink edges. Have each student fill out one of the cards.

For each tag, cut a 4½ x 2¾-inch piece from each of two printed papers and adhere them to each other, wrong sides facing. Embellish both sides of tag as desired with additional pieces of printed paper, rub-on transfers, stickers, paper flowers, silk flowers, brads, rhinestones, etc.; adhere a photo to one side and the "comment card" to the other. Punch a hole in one end of the tag; thread ribbon through hole and tie around the stem of a large silk flower. Arrange flowers in a vase. ■

SOURCES: Printed papers from My Mind's Eye; rub-on transfers from Doodlebug Design Inc.; stickers from K&Company.

Materials

Small color photos	Word stickers	Rhinestones	Paper adhesive
Card stock: assorted bright colors	Black ink pad	1½-inch-wide fuchsia ribbon	Computer and printer
Pink/lime/green printed papers	Paper flowers	Vase	
Rub-on transfers	Silk flowers	Silk flowers on stems	
	Brads: mini, decorative	Hole punch	

GOOFY BOYS

DESIGN BY SUSAN STRINGFELLOW

Capture fun-loving memories in an altered book filled with mini layouts.

Project note: Build layouts on card stock or printed paper cut to fit individual covers and pages. Stitch and embellish layouts before adhering completed layouts to book.

Front cover: Trace and cut blue card stock to cover front of board book. Tear one long edge of a 1½ x 5-inch strip of plaid paper; adhere strip vertically to layout near right edge with torn edge facing spine. Adhere rickrack over straight edge of paper strip; trim ends even. Machine-stitch around edges of layout ⅛ inch from edge, down torn edge of paper strip, and down center of rickrack using straight stitch and beige thread.

Using light green paint for ink, stamp "boys" down left edge of cover, positioning letters on their sides as shown; stamp asterisk over edge of "s" using light yellow paint. Adhere a 1 x ½-inch rectangle of brown swirls printed paper to upper left corner near top edge and left edges even. Apply dotted-outline heart, arrow and rectangle transfers over "boys"; using art pen, write "we luv … the … goofy" inside outlines and add dots along left and top edges of layout as shown in photo. Lightly ink surface of layout with sepia ink.

CONTINUED ON PAGE 167

Materials

- Digital photos or color photos approximately 3 x 3¾ inches
- 5-inch-square board book kit
- Photo paper (optional)
- Card stock: ivory, white (optional), blue, light blue, light green, gold, brown
- Brown/green/blue/cream printed paper: brown swirl, plaid, rings, floral, diamonds
- Stamps: small dotted circle, 2-inch lowercase alphabet

- Acrylic paints: light green and light yellow
- Sepia distress ink
- Ink pads: light blue, light green
- Black art pen
- Dotted-outline rub-on transfers
- Flat blue buttons: 1-inch round, 1-inch flower
- Brads: brown, mini blue, mini black
- Gold compass charm
- Craft stick

- 2¾-inch white silk flower
- 2½-inch embroidered flower embellishment
- Cream crochet thread or pearl cotton
- Brown rickrack
- Complementary ribbons
- ⅜-inch-wide twill trim: blue/beige striped, brown/white striped
- Small circle punch
- Die-cutting machine

- Dies: 2¼-inch flower, small file tab, tiny tag, tiny seed packet, photo corner
- Sewing machine
- Sewing thread: beige, brown
- Fine sandpaper
- Matte medium gel
- Computer with photo-editing program (optional)
- Printer (optional)

OUR FAMILY

DESIGN BY KRISTEN SWAIN

Celebrate family with a personalized, altered coin holder that's sure to become a treasured keepsake.

Project note: Ink edges of all pieces cut or punched from printed paper before adhering them to album.

Paint all surfaces of coin album. Cut rectangles from assorted printed papers to fit on covers and pages; ink edges and adhere to covers and pages.

Cover: Cut complementary printed paper to cover lower 4¾ inches of cover; adhere to cover with edges even. Cut 2¾-inch photo corners from two printed papers. Use computer to generate 4-inch initial of family name; cut initial from woven background floral printed paper. Adhere printed paper photo corners and initial to solid dark rust paper and cut out, leaving narrow borders. Adhere photo corners to upper right and lower left corner ⅛ inch from edges of printed paper; adhere initial to lower right corner ½ inch from right and bottom edges.

Attach square decorative brad to rust flower; adhere over seam between papers, near left edge. Staple a folded length of rickrack; adhere to left edge of initial.

Inner cover: Adhere a 4¼ x 5⅝-inch piece of solid light blue card stock over printed paper 1 inch from top. Cut 2-inch photo corners from two printed papers; adhere to solid dark rust paper and cut out, leaving narrow borders. Adhere two of the larger photos to inner cover at an angle as shown. Adhere large photo corners over upper left and upper right corners of upper and lower photos respectively; adhere kraft photo corners over remaining corners. Apply family-themed rub-on transfer to right of upper photo; top with brown ribbon bow. Adhere floral metal tile and knotted piece of blue ribbon to left of lower photo. Adhere burgundy ribbon across inner cover ¾ inch from bottom edge; attach silver ring and knot of light blue ribbon 1½ inches from right edge; attach mini brad through center of paper flower and adhere 1 inch from left edge.

Inner pages: Adhere remaining large photo and library pocket to pages where desired. Use craft knife to trim out

CONTINUED ON PAGE 166

Materials

Color photos: 3 (4 x 3-inch), assorted small (1-inch) photos

6 x 8-inch trifold coin album

Solid-color printed papers: blue, rust, light rust, light green

Rust/pink/blue/beige/green printed papers: white background floral, rust background floral, woven background floral, stripes

3 (2½ x 1¼-inch) tags

Small kraft photo corners

Library pocket

Slide mount

1½-inch paper flower

Rub-on transfers: black and white family-themed, alphabet

Alphabet stamps

Rust acrylic paint

Brown ink pad

Small buttons

Metal embellishments: heart, key, ¾-inch silver ring, white

1¾-inch fan, "Laugh" and "Happy," letters for name, initial dog tag, 1¼-inch square floral tile

Deep red safety pin

Antique mini brads

Decorative brads: square, round

¼- to ⅜-inch-wide ribbons: light blue, rust, brown, burgundy

Light blue rickrack

Silk flowers: 1¾-inch rust, 2½-inch white

1-inch burgundy leather flower

Paintbrush

Fine sandpaper

1¼-inch circle punch

Stapler with staples

Craft knife

Label maker with black label tape

Paper adhesive

Computer and printer

BUNDLE UP

DESIGN BY SHERRY WRIGHT

Snowflake printed papers are the perfect photo background on this wintry mini clipboard magnet.

Paint metal clip white. Adhere a 4½ x 3-inch piece of snowflake circles paper to clipboard with bottom and side edges even; trim paper to match clipboard's curved edges. With brown ink pad, ink long edges of two 4½ x 1-inch strips of snowflake squares paper. Adhere one piece across clipboard ⅝ inch from top edge; adhere second strip across clipboard ½ inch from bottom edge.

Tie two 8-inch strips of each ribbon through hole in clip. Ink edges of chipboard snowflake circle with brown ink pad and adhere to front of clip, holding piece in place for a minute to allow adhesive to set. Adhere chipboard "bundle up" to lower right corner of clipboard, ¼ inch from bottom and right edges.

Adhere magnet strips to reverse side of clipboard. Round corners of photo; secure under clipboard clip. ■

SOURCES: Printed papers and chipboard embellishments from Scenic Route Paper Co.; ribbons from KI Memories; adhesive from Beacon.

Materials

2⅞-inch-square color photo	Chipboard embellishments:	Brown ink pad	Self-adhesive magnet strips
4½ x 4¾-inch clipboard	"bundle up,"	⅜-inch-wide polka-dot	Foam brush
Snowflake printed papers:	snowflake circle	ribbons: white/blue,	Corner rounder punch
circles, squares	White paint	multicolor/light blue	Paper adhesive

PHOTO CUBE

DESIGN BY SHERRY WRIGHT

Coordinating papers dress up a premade photo cube to create a special gift package and photo display all in one.

With photo cube lying flat, measure sides (sides on sample are 5 inches square). Cut printed paper to size for each side, tracing center opening on reverse side of printed paper and cutting it out with a craft knife. With cube still lying flat, adhere paper to sides, mixing prints as desired.

Trim photos to fit in frame openings; adhere photos to reverse side of photo cube. *Option: Cut six 5-inch squares of card stock and adhere to reverse side of cube over* *frame openings, leaving top edges open; slide photos in and out of individual frames through open top edges.*

Fold cube and assemble according to manufacturer's instructions. Stamp family-themed sentiments onto coordinating stickers and adhere to photo cube as desired. ■

SOURCES: Photo cube from Fun Expressions; printed papers, stickers, stamps and ink from Paper Salon; adhesive from Beacon.

Materials

6 (4-inch-square) photos	*Printed paper:*	Family-themed stamps	Paper adhesive
Foldable photo cube	2 complementary prints	Coffee-bean ink	
Card stock (optional)	Card-stock stickers	Craft knife	

Materials

Black-and-white photos (see Project Note)

3 (5¼ x 10½-inch) paper bags

Pink card stock

Printed papers: pink/beige/brown striped, floral, polka-dot; solid beige

Pink/beige/brown card-stock stickers

Girl-themed vellum stickers

Pink die cuts: 1¾-inch flowers, ¾-inch round buckle

Foam stamps: 1½-inch alphabet, 3-inch flower

Acrylic paints: pink, light pink, brown

¼-inch-wide ribbons: white stitching on pink, white stitching on brown, brown-and-white gingham-checked, pink-and-white gingham-checked

Pink mini rickrack

Photo turns

Bronze mini brads

Paper clips: pink, white

Fine-tip pen (optional)

Foam brush

Staplers: mini, regular

Staples: magenta mini, silver regular

Sewing machine with white thread

Adhesive dots

Double-sided tape

Computer and printer

ALL ABOUT KATIE

DESIGN BY STEPHANIE BARNARD

A few simple embellishments of paper, paint and ribbon added to folded paper bags make a stylish album for your favorite photos.

Project note: *Sample project includes 14 photos ranging in size from 1¼ x 1⅞ inches to 2¾ x 4 inches.*

Album: Stack paper bags with edges even, alternating open and closed ends. Machine-stitch down center of bags using a straight stitch. Fold bags in half along stitching; machine-stitch through bags again ⅝ inch from original stitching, first using a straight stitch and a second time using a zigzag stitch. Paint edges of book and individual pages using pink and brown paints.

Cover: Using pink paint for ink, stamp name on a 4½ x 2⅝-inch piece of solid beige paper. Using pink and brown paints, paint edges of stamped paper, 2⅜ x 4¾-inch piece of striped paper, 4 x 1¼-inch piece of floral paper, and 1½-inch square and 3⁄16 x 2-inch strip of polka-dot paper. Staple corners of stamped paper with silver staples. Referring to photo throughout, adhere striped paper strip to cover next to stitching; adhere floral paper across cover near bottom edge, and polka-dot square in upper right corner; adhere name panel over other papers.

Adhere pink die-cut flower in upper left corner; affix pink photo turn over bottom edge of name panel with mini brad near right edge. Adhere narrow polka-dot strip across lower right corner; trim edges even. Fold two 2-inch pieces of stitched brown ribbon and one of stitched pink ribbon in half; using mini stapler and magenta staples, staple ribbons down upper right edge of name panel.

Pages: Cut accent blocks and strips cut from printed papers; paint edges with pink and/or brown paints. Adhere papers to pages with photos. Using paints as ink, stamp flowers on some pages, using pink for petals and brown for flower centers. Embellish pages with ribbon, rickrack, stickers and die cuts, piercing centers of flower die cuts with mini brads. Slide paper clips over edges of photos, printed paper blocks and pages as desired.

Journaling: Use computer to generate, or hand-print, journaling onto pink card stock to fit on page; paint edges of journaling panels with brown paint. ■

SOURCES: Printed paper, stickers, brads and ribbons from All My Memories; foam stamps from Making Memories; paints from Plaid Enterprises; die cuts from Ellison/Sizzix; adhesive dots and double-sided tape from Therm O Web.

Materials

Black-and-white digital photo or regular photo

7 x 5-inch primed, stretched canvas

Printable transparency (optional)

Printable canvas paper (optional)

Acrylic paints: green, light green, light blue, pink, cream, red, white

Rub-on transfers: black letters, dictionary page

Metal embellishments: ½-inch "LOVE" flower charm, ⅝-inch button

$^{11}/_{16}$-inch-square red acrylic hearts tile

Pink mini brad

3 small self-adhesive pink rhinestones

1-inch red pressed, preserved flower

Paintbrushes

Soft cloth

Adhesive applicator

Computer with photo-editing software

Printer

YOU ARE BEAUTIFUL

DESIGN BY EMILY DEISROTH

Brush strokes and swirls of paint add an artsy element to this canvas design.

Paint entire canvas green; when dry, repaint with light green, allowing a few streaks of darker green to show through. Paint designs on canvas as desired using remaining colors and painting sides of canvas. Sample is painted with a design of simple flowers and swirls, including a cream flower in the upper right corner.

Resize photo on computer to 2⅞ x 3¾ inches; print mirror image of photo onto transparency. Apply adhesive to rough side of transparency; adhere transparency to unprimed side of canvas paper. Using a soft cloth, gently rub over photo to remove air pockets. Trim around photo leaving ¼-inch borders. Draw blade of scissors across bottom edge of photo to roughen it. *Option: Use a regular black-and-white photo.*

Apply rub-on transfers to painted canvas as desired. Adhere photo to canvas, allowing it to overlap edge as desired. Thread mini brad through loop in flower charm; adhere to canvas in upper left corner. Adhere button in center of cream flower in upper right corner. Adhere preserved flower in lower left corner. Adhere acrylic tile and rhinestones in lower right corner.

SOURCES: Rub-on transfers from Making Memories and 7gypsies; transparency from 3M; canvas paper from Hewlett-Packard; paints from Golden Artist Colors Inc.; acrylic tile from KI Memories; rhinestones from Heidi Swapp/Advantus Corp.; adhesive applicator from Xyron.

ALTERED LETTER "K"

DESIGN BY STEPHANIE BARNARD

Team up your initial with some acrylic letter tiles and photos for a creative, personalized piece of artwork.

Project note: Adhere elements using double-sided tape unless instructed otherwise.

Paint all surfaces of "K" magenta. When dry, adhere printed paper to front of letter as shown, trimming edges even. Punch name from shrink plastic using alphabet dies; shrink according to manufacturer's instructions. Paint letters dark purple; Paint letters dark purple and adhere to "K" as shown.

Die-cut flower, mini tag and heart from printed papers. Paint edges of flowers; adhere flowers and heart to "K." Apply words using rub-on transfers as desired. Thread mini tag onto wire. Wrap wire around top of "K," curling ends as desired.

Adhere photo; tie ribbon in a bow around "K" as shown. Adhere three crystals to upper right edge of "K." ■

SOURCES: Papier-mâché letter from Darice; printed paper and rub-on transfers from All My Memories; shrink plastic from SHRINKY DINKS™; ink and paint from Plaid Enterprises/All Night Media; wire from Artistic Wire; rhinestones from Creative Crystals; paper flower from Prima; die-cutting machine and dies from Ellison/Sizzix; adhesive dots and double-sided tape from Therm O Web.

Materials

Small photo	Ink	3 crystal rhinestones	Dies: alphabet, flower,
8-inch papier-mâché "K"	Acrylic paints: magenta,	Paper flower	mini tag, heart
Printed papers	dark purple	Paintbrush	Adhesive dots
Shrink plastic	Complementary plastic-coated	Craft knife	Double-sided tape
Girl-themed rub-on transfers	wire	Die-cutting machine	

Winter Frost

CONTINUED FROM PAGE 128

Use jewel tool to adhere crystal to center of snowflake.

Adhere 6 x 4-inch photo to lower left corner of layout as shown. Flatten three bottle caps using rubber mallet or die-cutting machine with converter; set two aside. Adhere third bottle cap to upper right corner of 6 x 4-inch photo; adhere red snowflake sticker to bottle cap.

Adhere orange plaid printed paper to reverse side of "W winter" stencil; adhere stencil to center top of layout. Apply "Winter" and "Frost" rub-on transfers to upper right corner of layout; outline "Frost" with black marker. Center and affix snowflake brad to circle in upper right corner of layout. Attach pink paper clip to top right edge of layout.

File folder: Ink edges of die-cut file folder with embossing ink; sprinkle with embossing powder and emboss with heat tool. Turn folder on end; adhere a smaller photo (approximately 3¼ x 2⅝ inches) at an angle to upper left corner of folder front. Adhere ribbon photo corner to upper left corner of photo.

Fold 3-inch pieces of hot pink and gingham-checked ribbon in half; staple folds along left edge of "S snow" stencil. Clip red binder clip over right edge. Adhere stencil at an angle to lower right corner of folder front. Thread a 4-inch piece of gingham-checked ribbon through aqua button; knot ends on front and adhere button to upper right corner of file folder, next to photo.

Adhere halves of two 3-inch sections of hook-and-loop fastening tape to back of folder; adhere matching halves to right side of layout so that folder will be affixed at an angle 1¾ inches from bottom edge and 1¼ inches from right edge.

File pages: Sand edges of file pages. Adhere smaller photos to both sides of pages. Embellish pages as desired with stencils, stapled cuts of ribbon, card-stock stickers, buttons, remaining flattened bottle caps, snowflake spangles, crystals, paper clips and rub-on transfers. For color and texture, allow some ribbons, buttons and tabs to extend beyond edges of folder. Place file pages in folder;

hold folder closed with binder clip. Affix folder to layout with hook-and-loop strips. ■

SOURCES: Printed papers, file folder, stencils, card-stock stickers and transparency from Daisy D's Paper Co.; bottle cap stickers from Design Originals; rub-on transfers from Junkitz; embossing powder from Ranger Industries Inc.; marker from ZIG Memory System; ribbons and buttons from Doodlebug Design Inc.; photo corners, metal snowflake plaque, metal snowflake brad and mailbox tile from Making Memories; crystals and jewel-setting tool from Creative Crystal Co.; die-cutting machine with flattening converter from Ellison/Sizzix; embossing tool from EK Success Ltd.; adhesive from Beacon.

Our Family

CONTINUED FROM PAGE 157

circles where photos and embellishments will be positioned, leaving uncut areas to accommodate larger photo and library pocket; sand cut edges. Adhere small photos in openings. Adhere strips and rectangles of printed paper over untrimmed areas. Embellish remaining openings and surfaces of inner pages as desired; sample includes: stamped and rub-on transfer sentiments applied to punched circles of solid-color papers; sentiments printed on label maker; ribbon bows and knots; buttons; metal embellishments; family name spelled out with initial dog tag and individual metal letters; leather flower with mini brad in center; stapled cuts of assorted ribbons; silk flowers embellished with decorative brad, etc.

Library pocket: Adhere a 3¼ x 3⅛-inch piece of light rust solid-color paper and two small photos to contrasting printed paper and trim, leaving narrow borders. Adhere photos to light rust panel; add sentiments with label tape and rub-on transfers. Adhere photo panel to library pocket.

Tag: Fold a 1½ x 2¾-inch rectangle of contrasting printed paper over the top edge of a 3 x 5-inch tag cut from dark rust solid-color paper; attach with round decorative brad. Embellish tag with strips, rectangles and circles punched from printed papers. Adhere two small photos to printed paper and trim, leaving narrow borders. Adhere to tag at an angle, overlapping them as shown. Apply rub-on transfer sentiment to lower portion of tag. Slide tag into library pocket. ■

SOURCES: Coin album from Bazzill; printed paper from Chatterbox; photo corners from Canson; library pocket from Autumn Leaves; paper flower from The Natural Paper Co.; rub-on transfers from Li'l Davis Designs and Making Memories; stamps from PSX; paint from Delta; ink pad from Marvy Uchida; buttons, charms, silk flowers and safety pin from Craft Supply; decorative brads, metal letters, suede flower and ribbons from Making Memories; metal words from JoAnn's Scrap Essentials; metal sticker from Autumn Leaves; label maker from DYMO Corp.

Goofy Boys

CONTINUED FROM PAGE 155

Flower: Apply flower rub-on transfer to 1⅛-inch round button. Trim several individual swirls from brown swirls printed paper. Cut a 4-inch length of ribbon; fold in half. Cut a 2-inch length of rickrack; adhere ribbon and rickrack to lower right corner of cover, positioning so that ends of ribbon point up. Adhere 2¾-inch white silk flower to lower right corner of cover, overhanging bottom edge slightly and allowing ribbon to show above; adhere button to center of flower, tucking ends of paper swirls under button.

Tags: Die-cut three tags from ivory card stock; using art pen, write names on tags and add dotted outlines. Thread each tag onto a length of crochet thread that has been "distressed" with light blue ink; attach crochet threads to layout just to right of flower and near bottom edge using blue mini brad.

Adhere layout to front cover of board book. Adhere blue/beige striped twill binding over spine; trim ends even.

Photo pages: Cut card stock in desired colors to fit on individual pages. Adhere accent panels and strips cut from contrasting card stock or printed paper as desired. Machine-stitch around edges of layouts using straight and zigzag stitches as desired. Adhere ribbon tabs and rickrack to layouts before or after stitching, as desired.

Print a color photo measuring approximately 2¾ x 3¹³⁄₁₆ inches for each page, leaving a narrow white border. ***Option:*** *Adhere cropped color photos to white card stock and trim, leaving narrow borders.* Adhere a photo to each layout.

Photo page embellishments: Accent photos with die-cut photo corners of card stock or printed paper. Ink surfaces and/or edges of layouts with distress ink or medium gel as desired.

Apply dotted-outline rub-on transfers, overlapping photos as desired; using art pen, add titles and journaling within and around transfers, and repeat dotted pattern along edges of photo or layout.

Adhere punched circles or strips of printed paper or card stock; embellish with mini brads or rub-on transfers. Die-cut file tabs from card stock; add labels using art pen; adhere file tabs to edges of photos or individual layouts.

Attach lengths of ribbon or twill; embellish with mini brads, metal embellishments or charms.

Die-cut mini tags and seed packets from card stock or printed paper; add journaling using art pen. Thread tags on crochet thread that has been "distressed" with ink; tuck tags into envelopes and adhere to layouts.

Die-cut a 2¼-inch flower from printed paper; attach mini brad through center. Cover one surface of a craft stick with complementary printed paper; sand edges lightly and adhere flower to one end of craft-stick "stem"; adhere flower to layout.

Embellish buttons with punched circles of printed paper or rub-on transfers; adhere buttons to layouts.

Stamped pages: Using paints as ink, stamp names, numerals or words onto printed paper or card stock cut to fit pages. Embellish stamped pages as desired. ∎

SOURCES: Board book kit, embellishments and ribbons from Paperdillies; printed paper from Chatterbox and 3 Bugs in a Rug; stamps from Sugarloaf Products and Just for Fun; paints from Making Memories; distress inks from Ranger Industries Inc.; art pen from Faber Castell; rub-on transfers from Polar Bear Press; die-cutting machine and dies from QuicKutz Inc.; matte medium gel from Golden Artist Colors Inc.

Winter Beauty

CONTINUED FROM PAGE 61

Click on curved arrow beside color palette, changing foreground color to white. Select Rectangular Marquee tool in tool palette. Click just inside top left corner of image. Hold down left mouse button and drag to create box just inside edges. Right-click on image; click "Stroke" option. Adjust settings to read as follows: Width: 30 px; Location: inside; Blending Mode: normal; Opacity: 100 percent. Click "OK."

Open swirl stamp image. Click on curved arrow beside color palette, changing foreground color to blue. Click Paint Bucket tool in tool palette; click on image to fill with new color.

Select Move tool from tool palette. Click on image and hold down left mouse button to drag and drop swirl onto layout.

With photo area still highlighted, click "Layer" on main toolbar. Click "Arrange" option. Click on "Bring to Front" to bring photo to front of page. Hold down left mouse button and drag to top right corner. Click on corner adjustment mark on image.

Locate Scale tool along top of screen below main toolbar. Readjust height and width to 60 percent; set to "Rotate 30 degrees." Click check mark to confirm.

Click on swirl image to select. Click on "Layer" in main toolbar; click on "Duplicate Layer." Name image and click "OK" in pop-up window. Drag new copy of swirl just below border. Click on corner adjustment mark of image.

Locate Scale tool along top of screen below main toolbar. Readjust height and width to 60 percent; set to "Rotate 90 degrees." Click check mark to confirm.

Open blue brad image. With image selected, click on "Enhance" option in main toolbar. Select "Adjust Color" option; click on "Color Variations." With "Intensity" set at midlevel, select "Midtones" option. Click three times on the "Darken" feature; click "OK."

Select Move tool from tool palette. Drag and drop brad image onto main layout. With brad area still highlighted, click "Layer" on main toolbar. Click "Arrange" option. Click on "Bring to Front" to bring brad to front of page. Hold left mouse button and drag brad image just above top left corner of photo. Click on "Layer" option in the main toolbar. Click on "Duplicate Layer" function. In pop-up window, name new layer and click "OK."

Repeat to create a total of three brads. Hold right mouse button and drag brads into a horizontal line.

Select Text tool in tool palette; set text to 95-pt. Vivaldi. Click on image to begin title; type text and click check mark at top of screen to confirm.

Select Move tool from tool palette; click on title to select. In "Styles and Effect" window, select the "Layer Styles" and "Bevel" drop-down options. Click on "Simple Emboss" feature.

Click "File" function in main toolbar; select "Save As" option and save file.

Print image. ■

SOURCES: Holiday Magic digital printed paper and images from www.shabbyprincess.com; Photoshop Elements from Adobe Systems Inc.

Blow Out Your Candle

CONTINUED FROM PAGE 97

and cut circle around journaling. Adhere journaling to layout ⅜ inch from right edge and 1¼ inches from top edge of layout, overlapping ribbon and bottom edge of top orange floral strip. Attach 4 mini brads through ribbon, placing one at each end; then placing the remaining two between the left-side brad and the journaling circle.

Adhere three smaller photos to white card stock and trim, leaving ⅛-inch borders. Arrange photos on layout, positioning one just to left of journaling. Adhere remaining photo-mounting corner over lower left corner of photo at bottom left. Photo in lower right corner may be slightly tilted and edge trimmed even with edge of layout.

Adhere 1-inch white card-stock circle to layout 1 inch from right edge and ¼ inch from bottom edge. Snap shank off button; adhere to card-stock circle using craft cement. Tear paper from center of remaining metal-rim tag; thread rim onto ribbon and adhere ribbon across layout from right edge to edge of photo, 1⅜ inches from bottom edge of layout; position tag over circle and button.

Attach mini brads through ends of ribbon and adhere tag to layout. ∎

SOURCES: Printed paper from Chatterbox; rub-on transfers from Making Memories; stamps from Hero Arts Rubber Stamps; buttons from Jesse James & Co. Inc.; ribbons from Li'l Davis Designs; circle punch from Marvy; circle cutter from Provo Craft/Coluzzle.

Beachcomber

CONTINUED FROM PAGE 106

To make ribbon look like it has been run under the opposite side of the straight pin head, use the Eraser tool and select the small, round, hard brush. Click "View," then "Zoom" to enlarge the area of the photo as much as possible. Make sure that ribbon layer is selected in layers palette. Using Eraser, very carefully erase the ribbon along the rounded edge of the head of the pin. *Note: If you erase too much, use "Edit," "Step Backward" or the History palette.*

Open "ribbons" folder and select the "dots" ribbon; drag it to your layout. Rotate ribbon to vertical by going to "Edit," "Transform," "Rotate90CW." Position ribbon on left side of layout. Click "Ctrl-[" as many times as necessary to place ribbon behind large layer of printed paper at bottom of layout.

Repeat the previous procedure with ribbons labeled "dots1" and "stripes2."

Title: Choose Text tool from toolbox and click on layout; you should see a blinking line where the text will begin. Size desired font at 150pt and set foreground color in toolbox to black; type "BEACH." Use Move tool to position word on layout, below photo.

Add a new layer by going to "Layer," "New," "Layer" and click "OK." Repeat previous step to add "comber" to layout, first appying settings for a 60pt script-style font and setting foreground color to white.

To give your layout a faded, weathered look, choose the Dodge tool from the toolbox and select the soft round brush at approximately 350 px; set exposure to 50 percent. Click on selected layers within Layers palette to choose papers you would like to dodge. Dodge areas most likely to fade and weather in real life, including corners and edges of paper.

Within "elements" folder, open "transparent elements" folder. Open hibiscus shapes labeled "flower1," "flower3" and "flower5." Use Move tool to click and drag each flower to layout; group them in upper left corner of layout. *Note: These are the only elements to which you should not add a Drop Shadow.*

Within "elements" folder, open "tags" folder. Open each tag and drag to your layout, positioning them in a column to left of title. Arrange tags as desired using the "Edit," "Transform," "Rotate"; "Ctrl-["; or "Ctrl-]" techniques.

Add journaling to tabs using the Text tool and desired 12pt sans serif font with foreground color set to black. Add a new layer by going to "Layer," "New," "Layer" and click "OK." Add date to upper left corner of layout using Text tool and 24pt sans serif font.

Select Brush tool from Layers palette. In Photoshop browser, click small arrow next to brush icon to open the brush preset picker. When window opens, click arrow in upper right corner, then select "load brushes." Use browser to locate the "Rhonna Farrer," "Rhonna Swirls ABR" file; click "load" to load brushes in palette. Select brush 1474.

Go to "Layer," "New," "Layer" and click "OK." With foreground color set to black, click selected brush once at upper right corner of layout. Select brush 1401; click once in various places along bottom and left sides of layout.

Add a new layer by going to "Layer," "New," "Layer" and click "OK." Download the "Michelle Coleman," "Brush Strokes ABR" file. Select brush 1901 at 2500 px. With foreground color set to white, click brush once in upper right corner of layout. Using same settings, select brushes 2036 and 2144 and click in their respective corners of layout. Use "Ctrl-[" to move this layer until it appears behind the journaling tags.

Save layout and print. ∎

SOURCES: Tropical Breeze digital printed paper and elements by Michelle Underwood from Scrapbook Bytes; digital Rhonna Swirls brushes by Rhonna Farrer from Two Peas In a Bucket Inc.; Brush Strokes brushes by Michelle Coleman from Scrap Artist; Photoshop from Adobe Systems Inc.

'50 Ford

CONTINUED FROM PAGE 117

'50 Ford Flourish
Enlarge pattern 118%.

Seasons

CONTINUED FROM PAGE 141

Seasons Leaf Templates

Learning to Skate

CONTINUED FROM PAGE 92

stock; center and adhere over circles printed-paper strip ⅝ inch from right edge.

Adhere remaining portion of 5 x 7-inch photo to right page so that it aligns with image on left page. Using a teal mini brad, attach photo turn over edge of photo near lower right corner. Adhere a 2½ x 3¼-inch photo to upper right corner of layout ¼ inch from right edge with top edges even.

Adhere a 6 x ¼-inch strip of surfboard printed paper to blue card stock; trim, leaving narrow borders along top and bottom edges and trimming edges even on ends. Adhere across top of layout so that ends align with matching strip on left page.

Lightly sand edges of a 1¾ x 3-inch rectangle of blue card stock; adhere to lower right corner of layout. Adhere a 2½ x 3¼-inch photo to layout beside blue rectangle with bottom edges of photo and rectangle even. Adhere a 2 x ½-inch strip of blue card stock and a 4½ x ¾-inch strip of surfboards printed paper across bottom of layout so that left ends align with ends of matching strips on left page. Attach orange and dark blue mini brads to tan card stock at right end of blue card-stock strip.

Lightly sand gold alphabet and numeral stickers; adhere stickers to spell "Age" on blue circle; adhere stickers for year on blue rectangle at lower right corner. ■

SOURCES: Printed papers and stickers from Arctic Frog; mini brads and photo turns from Creative Impressions.

GENERAL INSTRUCTIONS
Paper crafting is easy, creative and fun. Collect basic tools and supplies, learn a few simple terms and techniques, and you're ready to start. The possibilities abound!

Cutting and Tearing

Craft knife, cutting mat Must-have tools. Mat protects work surface, keeps blades from getting dull.

Measure and mark Diagrams show solid lines for cutting, dotted lines for folding.

Other cutters Guillotine and rotary-blade paper cutters, oval and circle cutters, cutters that cut unusual shapes via a gear or cam system, swivel-blade knives that cut along the channels of plastic templates, and die cutting machines (large or small in size and price). Markers that draw as they cut.

Punches Available in hundreds of shapes and sizes ranging from $1/16$ inch to over 3 inches (use for eyelets, lettering, dimensional punch art, and embellishments). Also punches for two-ring, three-ring, coil, comb and disk binding.

Scissors Long and short blades that cut straight or a pattern. Scissors with nonstick coating are ideal for cutting adhesive sheets and tape, bonsai scissors best for cutting rubber or heavy board. Consider comfort—large holes for fingers, soft grips.

Tearing Tear paper for collage, special effects, layering on cards, scrapbook pages and more. Wet a small paintbrush; tear along the wet line for a deckle edge.

Embellishments

If you are not already a pack rat, it is time to start! Embellish projects with stickers, eyelets, brads, nail heads, wire, beads, iron-on ribbon and braid, memorabilia and printed ephemera.

Embossing

Dry embossing Use a light source, stencil, card stock and stylus tool. Add color or leave raised areas plain.

Heat embossing Use embossing powder, ink, card stock and a heat tool to create raised designs and textures.

Powders Come in a wide range of colors. Fine grain is called "detail" and heavier called "ultrathick." Embossing powders will not stick to most dye inks—use pigment inks or special clear embossing inks for best results.

Glues and Adhesives

Basics Each glue or adhesive is formulated for a particular use or specified surfaces. Read the label and carefully follow directions, especially for glues that could endanger personal safety.

Foam tape Adds dimension.

Glue dots, adhesive sheets and cartridge type machines Quick grab, no drying time needed.

Glue pens Fine line control.

Glue sticks Wide coverage.

Repositionable products Useful for stencils and temporary holding.

Measuring

Rulers A metal straightedge for cutting with a craft knife (a must-have tool). Match the length of the ruler to the project (shorter rulers are easier to use when working on smaller projects).

Quilter's grid ruler Use to measure squares and rectangles.

Pens and Markers

Choose inks (permanent, watercolor, metallic, etc.), **colors** (sold by sets or individually), and **nibs** (fine point, calligraphy, etc.) **to suit the project.** For journals and scrapbooks, make sure inks are permanent and fade-resistant.

Store pens and markers flat unless the manufacturer says otherwise.

Scoring and Folding

Folding Mountain folds—up, valley folds—down. Most patterns will have different types of dotted lines to denote mountain or valley folds.

Tools Scoring tool and bone folder. Fingernails will scar the surface of the paper.

Paper and Card Stock

Card stock Heavier and stiffer than paper. A sturdy surface for cards, boxes, ornaments.

Paper Lighter weight surface used for drawing, stamping, collage.

Storage and organization Store paper flat and away from moisture. Arrange by color, size or type. Keep your scraps for collage projects.

Types Handmade, milled, marbled, mulberry, origami, embossed, glossy, matte, botanical inclusions, vellum, parchment, preprinted, tissue and more.

Stamping

Direct-to-paper (DTP) Use ink pad, sponge or stylus tool to apply ink instead of a rubber stamp.

Inks Available in pads and re-inker bottles. Types include dye and pigment, permanent, waterproof and fade resistant or archival, chalk finish, fast drying, slow drying, rainbow and more. Read the labels to determine what is best for a project or surface.

Make stamps Carve rubber, erasers, carving blocks, vegetables. Heat Magic Stamp foam blocks to press against textures. Stamp found objects such as leaves and flowers, keys and coins, etc.

Stamps Sold mounted on wood, acrylic or foam, or unmounted (rubber part only), made from vulcanized rubber, acrylic or foam.

Store Flat and away from light and heat.

Techniques Tap the ink onto the stamp (using the pad as the applicator) or tap the stamp onto the ink pad. Stamp with even hand pressure (no rocking) for best results. For very large stamps, apply ink with a brayer. Color the surface of a stamp with watercolor markers (several colors), huff with breath to keep the colors moist, then stamp; or lightly spray with water mist before stamping for a very different effect.

Unmounted stamps Mount temporarily on acrylic blocks with Scotch® Poster Tape or one of the other methods (hook and loop, paint on adhesives, cling plastic).

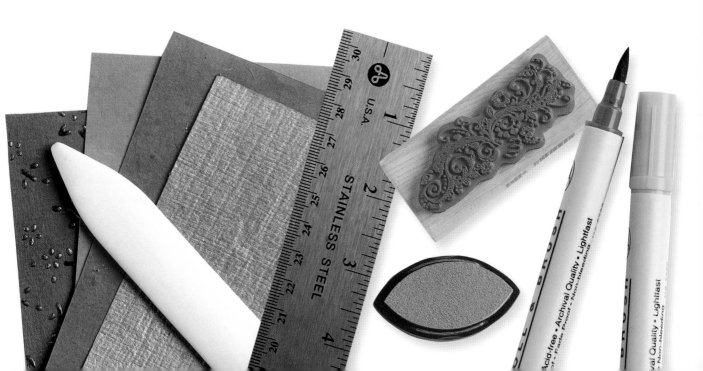

BUYER'S GUIDE

Projects in this book were made using products provided by the manufacturers listed below. Look for the suggested products in your local craft- and art-supply stores. If unavailable, contact suppliers below. Some may be able to sell products directly to you; others may be able to refer you to retail sources.

3M
(888) 364-3577
www.3m.com

7gypsies
(877) 7GYPSY7
www.sevengypsies.com

A Cherry on Top
(888) 381-9399
www.acherryontop.com

Adobe Systems Inc.
www.adobe.com

AAM
(888) 553-1998
www.allmymemories.com

AMACO (American Art Clay Co.)
(800) 374-1600
www.amaco.com

American Crafts
(801) 226-0747
www.americancrafts.com

American Traditional Designs
(800) 488-6656
www.americantraditional.com

Ampad
(800) 426-1368
www.ampad.com

Anna Griffin Inc.
(888) 817-8170
www.annagriffin.com

Arctic Frog
(479) 636-3764
www.arcticfrog.com

Around the Block Products
(801) 593-1946
www.aroundtheblockproducts.com

Artistic Wire Ltd.
(630) 530-7567
www.artisticwire.com

Autumn Leaves
(800) 588-6707
www.autumnleaves.com

BasicGrey
(801) 544-1116
www.basicgrey.com

Bazzill Basics Paper Inc.
(480) 558-8557
www.bazzillbasics.com

Beacon Adhesives Inc.
(914) 699-3400
www.beaconcreates.com

The Beadery
(401) 539-2432
www.TheBeadery.com

Better Homes and Gardens
www.bhg.com

Bitsy's PaperDillies
www.paperdillies.com

Bo-Bunny Press
(801) 771-4010
www.bobunny.com

Canon
www.canon.com

Canson
www.canson.com

Carl
www.carl-products.com

Carolee's Creations & Co.
(435) 563-1100
www.caroleescreations.com

Center City Designs/
Imagination Project Inc.
(888) 477-6532
www.imaginationproject.com

Chatterbox Inc.
(888) 416-6260
www.chatterboxinc.com

Cherry Arte
(212) 465-3495
www.cherryarte.com

Clearsnap Inc.
(888) 448-4862
www.clearsnap.com

Cloud 9 Design
(866) 348-5661
www.cloud9design.biz

Colorbök
(800) 366-4660
www.colorbok.com

Coluzzle/Provo Craft
(800) 937-7686
www.coluzzle.com

Creating Keepsakes
www.creatingkeepsakes.com

Creative Co-op Inc.
(866) 323-2264
www.creativecoopinc.com

Creative Crystal Co.
(800) 578-0716
www.creativecrystal.com

Creative Imaginations
(800) 942-6487
www.cigift.com

Creative Impressions
(719) 596-4860
www.creativeimpressions.com

dafont.com
www.dafont.com

Daisy D's Paper Co.
(888) 601-8955
www.daisydspaper.com

Dani Mogstad
www.designbydani.com

Darice Inc.
(866) 432-7423
www.darice.com

Delish Designs
www.delishdesigns.com

Delta Creative
(800) 423-4135
www.deltacrafts.com

Design Originals
(817) 877-7820|
www.d-originals.com

The DigiChick
www.thedigichick.com

DMD
www.dmdpaper.com

Dolphin Enterprises
(877) 910-3306
www.protect-a-page.com

Doodlebug Design Inc.
www.doodlebug.ws

DYMO Corp.
global.dymo.com

EK Success Ltd.
(800) 524-1349
www.eksuccess.com

Ellison/Sizzix
(800) 253-2238
www.ellison.com

Epson
www.epson.com

Eyelet Outlet
(618) 622-9741
www.eyeletoutlet.com

EZ Laser Designs
(423) 318-9676
www.ezlaserdesigns.com

Faber-Castell
(800) 642-2288
www.faber-castell.us

Family Treasures www.
familytreasures.com

Fancy Pants
www.fancypantsdesigns.com

Fibers By The Yard
(405) 364-8066
www.fibersbytheyard.com

Fiskars
(800) 500-4849
www.fiskars.com

FoofaLa
www.foofala.com

Fredrix Artist Canvas
www.fredrixartistcanvas.com

Gin-X/Imagination Project Inc.
(888) 477-6532
www.imaginationproject.com

Glue Dots International
(888) 688-7131
www.gluedots.com

Golden Artist Colors Inc.
(800) 959-6543
www.goldenpaints.com

Grafix Plastics
www.grafixplastics.com

Graham & Brown
(800) 554-0887
www.grahambrown.com

Heidi Grace Designs Inc.
(866) 348-5661
www.heidigrace.com

Heidi Swapp/Advantus Corp.
(904) 482-0092
www.heidiswapp.com

Hero Arts Rubber Stamps
(800) 822-4376
www.heroarts.com

Hewlett-Packard
www.hp.com

Holly McCaig Designs
www.hollymccaigdesigns.com

Jen Wilson
www.jenwilsondesigns.com

Jesse James & Co. Inc./ Dress It Up!
(610) 435-7899
www.jessejamesbeads.com

Jo-Ann Stores
www.joann.com

Junkitz
(732) 792-1108
www.junkitz.com

Just Rite Stampers/
Millennium Marking Co.
www.justritestampers.com

K&Company
(888) 244-2083
www.kandcompany.com

Karen Foster Design
(801) 451-9779
www.karenfosterdesign.com

KI Memories
(972) 243-5595
www.kimemories.com

Li'l Davis Designs
www.lildavisdesigns.com

Magic Scraps
(904) 482-0092
www.magicscraps.com

Magnetic Poetry
(800) 370-7697
www.magneticpoetry.com

Maisy Mo Designs
(973) 907-7262
www.maisymo.com

Making Memories
(801) 294-0430
www.makingmemories.com

Mara-Mi Inc.
(800) 627-2648
www.mara-mi.com

Marvy/Uchida of America
(800) 541-5877
www.uchida.com

May Arts & Craft Supply
www.mayarts.com

me & my BIG ideas
www.meandmybigideas.com

Microsoft
www.microsoft.com

Midwest Design Imports
(402) 691-8009
www.midwestdesignimports.com

Mom's Corner for Kids
www.momscorner4kids.com

Mustard Moon
(763) 493-5157
www.mustardmoon.com

My Mind's Eye Inc.
(866) 989-0320
www.mymindseye.com

The Natural Paper Co.
(734) 418-0796
www.naturalpapercompany.com

Nunn Design
(800) 761-3557
www.nunndesign.com

Offray & Son Inc.
www.offray.com

The Paper Adventures
(973) 406-5000
www.anwcrestwood.com

The Paper Co.
(973) 406-5000
www.anwcrestwood.com

Paper House Productions
(800) 255-7316
www.paperhouseproductions.com

The Paper Loft
(801) 254-1961
www.paperloft.com

Paper Salon Inc.
(800) 627-2648
www.papersalon.com

Paper Studio
www.paperstudio.com

Pebbles Inc.
(801) 235-1520
www.pebblesinc.com

Plaid Enterprises/All Night Media
(800) 842-4197
www.plaidonline.com

PM Designs
(888) 595-2887
www.designsbypm.com

Polar Bear Press
(801) 451-7670
www.polarbearpress.com

Pressed Petals
(800) 748-4656
www.pressedpetals.com

Prima Marketing Inc.
(909) 627-5532
www.primamarketinginc.com

PSX
www.sierra-enterprises.com

Purple Onion Designs
www.purpleoniondesigns.com

Queen & Co.
www.queenandco.com

QuicKutz Inc.
(888) 702-1146
www.quickutz.com

Ranger Industries Inc.
(732) 389-3535
www.rangerink.com

Royal & Langnickel
(800) 247-2211
www.royalbrush.com

Sakura Hobby Craft Inc.
(310) 212-7878
www.sakuracraft.com

Scenic Route Paper Co.
(801) 225-5754
www.scenicroutepaper.com

ScrapArtist.com
www.scrapartist.com

Scrapbook Bytes
(607) 642-5391
www.scrapbook-bytes.com

Scrappin' Sports 'N More
(435) 245-6044
www.qbaroo.com/scrappinsports/
website/selectgallery.cfm

Scrapworks Inc.
(801) 363-1010
www.scrapworks.com

SEI
(800) 333-3279
www.shopsei.com

Shabby Princess
www.shabbyprincess.com

Shrinky Dinks™
(262) 966-0305
www.shrinkydinks.com

Stickopotamus/EK Success Ltd.
(800) 524-1349
www.eksuccess.com

Sugarloaf Products Inc.
(770) 484-0722
www.sugarloafproducts.com

Suze Weinberg Design Studio
(732) 493-1390
www.schmoozewithsuze.com

Sweet Shoppe Designs
www.sweetshoppedesigns.com

Technique Tuesday
www.techniquetuesday.com

Teters
(800) 999-5996
www.teters.com

Therm O Web
(847) 520-5200
www.thermoweb.com

Three Bugs in a Rug
(801) 804-6657
www.3bugsinarug.com

Top Line Creations
(866) 954-0559
www.topline-creations.com

Tsukineko Inc.
(800) 769-6633
www.tsukineko.com

Two Peas In a Bucket Inc.
(888) TWO-PEAS
www.twopeasinabucket.com

Urban Lily
www.urbanlily.com

Wacom
(800) 922-9348
www.wacom.com

Wallies
(800) 766-3610, ext 485
www.wallies.com

We R Memory Keepers
(877) 742-5937
www.wermemorykeepers.com

Xyron
(800) 793-3523
www.xyron.com

ZIG Memory System/EK Success
(800) 524-1349
www.eksuccess.com

A New Beginning, p.98

DESIGNER PROJECT INDEX